London,
22.1.80

Kathie Webber's Book of
Spring Cooking

Kathie Webber's Book of
Spring Cooking

ELM TREE BOOKS · LONDON

First published in Great Britain in 1978 by
Elm Tree Books/Hamish Hamilton Ltd
90 Great Russell Street
London WC1B 3PT
and
Sphere Books Ltd
30/32 Gray's Inn Road
London WC1X 8JL

Jacket photograph by Mike Leale
Illustrations by Su Turner

British Library Cataloguing in Publication Data
Webber, Kathie
   Kathie Webber's book of Spring cooking.
   1. Cookery
   I. Book of Spring cooking
   641.5   TX652

   ISBN 0 241 89818 8

Printed in Great Britain by
Billing & Sons Ltd,
Guildford, Worcester and London

Contents

Kathie Webber's Book of
Spring Cooking

Metric Measurements

Metric measurements may vary from recipe to recipe, and it is essential to follow *either* imperial *or* metric measures throughout any one recipe. It's perfectly possible to specify 8-oz quantities in two recipes and have one convert to 200 g and the other to 225 g; this is of particular importance with, for example, pastry, where exact quantities are necessary to achieve the correct flour/fat ratio.

Another discrepancy, you may think, occurs when I've specified larger amounts of food than one would normally buy by the pound or half-pound. Nowadays we ask for ½ lb of tomatoes, not 7 oz (which may be what we want for a recipe) and in future we shall probably ask for a ½ kilo (kg) rather than 450 g. Half a kilo is a little more than 1 lb, but where the slight difference in weight won't alter the recipe, for instance, Broccoli with Butter, or Fish Crumble, I've given a metric quantity as you'd buy it.

Introduction

This book is one of four concerned with seasonal cookery and with the true appreciation of each ingredient that comes into our kitchens at its peak, having matured, ripened or simply become abundant because it's time to perpetuate the life-cycle again. Usually foods at the height of their season are not only in superb condition but also, because all beans fatten at once, all gooseberries ripen at once, they are plentiful in the markets and at their lowest prices – something to take advantage of.

Freezers, bless them, have given a whole new dimension to cookery. A freezer makes it easier to prepare soups from home-made stock, and left-overs (which at the time are just a nuisance and often thrown away because we're fed up with eating the same old thing) may be tucked into the cabinet to emerge later when they suggest some different use. Any glut of fruit or vegetables from garden or allotment used to mean a week in mid-July of standing in a hot and steamy kitchen bottling and making jams and jellies. Now we can freeze them first (a swift process) and at our leisure and own pace turn them into preserves of another kind.

But freezers have also blurred the seasons, too much I think. Once-seasonal foods are now available all the year round. I hate the idea of freezing rosebuds in June to decorate the Christmas table. I don't want to eat raspberries in November because the fresh fruit in July seems like a gift. Anticipating its appearance is followed by the almost ritualistic pleasure of preparing the first bowl – plump red fruit, sprinkled with fine sugar and hidden under thick golden cream from Devon. It's the same with mussels, redcurrants, Spring lamb and all the other friends who pay us a fleeting visit, rather like exotic migrant birds, only to depart for another year. By all means, though, freeze meat, fish, sausages, pies and poultry (peep in my freezer and you'll see it contains exactly these foods, though you'll also notice a vast quantity of home-cooked produce).

This volume is a celebration of all that Spring has to offer. Not the Spring of the calendar, or the newspapers declaring the first day of the season, or even the weather men, but a cook's Spring, the time when one says goodbye to the rich stews, casseroles and steamed puddings of a cold Winter and welcomes in their stead the new potatoes and early peas which indicate it's time to think about lighter dishes for the warmer days.

As March blusters to a close and April brings the first sunshine, new lamb comes into the butchers' shops along with poussins and delicious duckling. The fishmongers' slabs begin to hint at the varieties the fishermen will bring into our ports in the months to come and the greengrocers' displays lose their fir green and golden Winter look and take on a pale dusty beige and delicate green hue. Chickens get that Spring feeling and produce dozens of eggs, so this is the time to preserve and pickle them and use them in puddings and pancakes. Festivals in this three-month section of the cook's year are Easter and Shrove Tuesday or Pancake Day. To accompany our own familiar fare, I've included recipes and information from other countries to give a broad picture of how other people celebrate these important events in the Christian calendar. Salad greens begin to sprout in the gardens and the first glasshouse-grown foods appear; they're included here together with some nice dressings.

Fruit isn't too plentiful yet, but we do have the first gooseberries and bright pink and spindly rhubarb, which later will mature to a ruby-red, with fat, tart stalks standing proud in the garden, their wide canopies forming shelter for Charlie the cat. Both these fruits make good pickles and chutneys as well as jams and both sweet and savoury jellies to serve with meats. Lemon curd should be made in the Spring for lemons are plentiful and, like eggs, the other main ingredient of this curd, relatively cheap. You'll find lemons are used here in all manner of interesting dishes. Puddings and sponges are included, particularly those which take advantage of fresh ingredients.

This book is one of a series of four written to help you make the most of all the fresh produce when it's in season. The others – Summer, Autumn and Winter cookery – tell the story of the other seasons and all together they'll provide a year-round compendium containing dozens of interesting ways of preparing foods at their best and cheapest for good eating.

Kathie Webber

Vegetables

Although there's little in our gardens in March – the last of the sprouts, some Savoy cabbage and sprouting broccoli – tiny new potatoes are coming into the greengrocers, and through the month the supply of bright new carrots and Spring greens steadily improves.

Towards the end of the season, peas make their entrance, as do courgettes and mange tout, the flat pea pods, with peas inside as yet unformed, that are eaten complete as a sweet vegetable. Spinach, too, should be around and besides making a good vegetable or a base for egg and fish dishes under a rich sauce, it also makes an unusual salad. Jerusalem artichokes, knobbly tubers looking for all the world like misshapen potatoes, are delicious and if you've ignored them because you've heard how difficult they are to peel and how they go brown before you've managed it, forget all this. I never peel mine before cooking and I don't use lemon juice (not always convenient) or vinegar (don't like the taste on the artichokes) as many cooks suggest. Instead, I scrub them to remove the dirt, trim away the knobbliest bits, and drop them into a pan of salted water which prevents the cut edges from browning as effectively as the lemon juice or vinegar. When cooked, they're easy to peel, but like little new boiled potatoes, the skin is good to eat.

The first asparagus also arrives. 'Sparrow grass' they used to call it in the old Covent Garden market. I'm sure they still do, even though the market has moved across the river, but somehow the clean, organised complex isn't conducive to the retention of these old-fashioned names.

Peas with Mint

1.5 kg (3 lb) peas   pepper
salt   3 sprigs of mint
knob of butter

Shell the peas and rinse them under running cold water. Drop them into boiling salted water and cook them for 15 minutes or until tender but not squashy. Drain well, then toss them in the butter over a gentle heat. Sprinkle with black pepper and serve garnished with the mint sprigs.

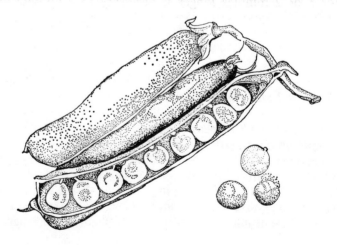

You may add the mint to the peas when they are boiling but I find the flavour of mint too strong for these new, tender and sweet peas.

Serves 6

Peas and Lettuce

100 g (4 oz) butter	5 ml (1 level teaspoon)
1.5 kg (3 lb) peas, prepared	sugar
1 small onion, finely	salt
chopped	pepper
1 small crisp lettuce,	
shredded	

Melt the butter in a large saucepan with 125 ml ($\frac{1}{4}$ pint) water. Add the peas, onion and lettuce, then sprinkle on the sugar and a good pinch of salt. Cover the pan tightly and cook the peas gently for about 10 minutes, shaking the pan frequently to make sure that the liquid doesn't completely evaporate and the peas stick to the bottom and burn. Remove the lid when the peas are just tender then cook them for 1 or 2 minutes longer if necessary to evaporate any remaining liquid. Sprinkle with a little pepper and serve.

Serves 6

Garden Peas Purée

175 g (6 oz) podded peas	salt
1 small onion, finely	pepper
chopped	5 ml (1 level teaspoon) mint,
50 g (2 oz) butter	finely chopped

Put the peas, onion, butter and 45 ml (3 tablespoons) cold water in a saucepan. Season with salt and pepper and bring to the boil, then cover the pan and cook gently until most of the liquid has been absorbed by the peas. Check the pan frequently and add another 15 ml (1 tablespoon) cold water if the peas look as though they will burn before they become tender. Blend the contents of the pan to a purée and return it to the pan. If your purée is too runny to hold its shape, stir in a little instant potato until the texture is right. Whisk the purée while you heat it through, and serve sprinkled with the mint.

Serves 4

Broccoli with Butter

| 1 kg (2 lb) broccoli | 100 g (4 oz) butter, melted |
| salt | freshly ground black pepper |

Wash the broccoli and trim the stalk ends. Divide the heads into florets about 5 cm (2 in) in diameter. Put the spears into fast-boiling salted water and cook them for about 7 minutes or until they are tender but not collapsing. Drain very well and serve with melted butter poured over the florets. Sprinkle with freshly ground black pepper.

Serves 6

Broccoli au Gratin

0.75 kg (1½ lb) broccoli, prepared
salt

Béchamel sauce:
25 g (1 oz) butter
25 g (1 oz) plain flour

250 ml (½ pint) milk
pepper
ground nutmeg
75 g (3 oz) unsalted butter
50 g (2 oz) fresh white breadcrumbs

Cook the broccoli in boiling salted water for about 7 minutes until just tender.

While it cooks, make the béchamel sauce. Melt the butter in a pan, stir in the flour and cook for 1 minute. Remove from the heat and gradually stir in the milk. Bring to the boil, stirring all the time, and cook the sauce for 2 minutes. Season with salt and pepper and some nutmeg.

Drain the broccoli and put the spears in a fireproof dish. Coat with the sauce. Melt 50 g (2 oz) of the unsalted butter, mix it with the breadcrumbs and sprinkle this mixture over the sauce. Dot with the remaining butter, sprinkle with a little pepper and put the dish under a hot grill until the crumbs are golden brown.

Serves 8

Broccoli 'a Crudo'

0.75 kg (1½ lb) broccoli, prepared
salt
45 ml (3 tablespoons) cooking oil

1 clove garlic, finely chopped
pepper
125 ml (¼ pint) dry white wine

Keep any small tender leaves when you prepare the broccoli and divide the heads into small florets. Leave the heads soaking in salted water. Heat the oil in a heavy pan and fry the garlic until it is golden, then add the broccoli leaves,

season with salt and pepper and cook gently until the leaves
are tender. Drain the broccoli heads well and add them to
the pan. Pour in the wine and 125 ml (¼ pint) cold water.
Bring slowly to the boil and cook gently, stirring occasionally, until the broccoli is tender.

Serves 4

Jerusalem Artichokes

0.5 kg (1 lb) Jerusalem   salt
   artichokes   pepper

Scrub the artichokes under running cold water and scrape
away or peel any discoloured patches. There is no need to
remove all the skin, a difficult task with these knobbly tubers,
because it's good to eat. Cut them into even-sized pieces and
drop them into salted cold water which will prevent the cut
surfaces from turning brown. When ready to cook them,
bring to the boil and boil gently for 15 to 20 minutes or until
tender. Drain. If you wish to remove the skin, now is the
time to do it. It's an easy job after cooking, but almost
impossible before. Season with pepper and serve.

Serves 6

Artichoke Fritters

1 kg (2 lb) Jerusalem
  artichokes, prepared
500 ml (1 pint) chicken
  stock
2 large eggs

salt
pepper
175 g (6 oz) fresh white
  breadcrumbs
oil for deep frying

Parboil the artichokes in the chicken stock for 5 minutes or until they are just tender but still crisp. Drain them well. Beat the eggs on a plate with a pinch each of salt and pepper. Cut the artichokes into thick slices and coat each slice first in egg, then in breadcrumbs, patting them on well. Shake off any extra crumbs. Heat the oil to 191°C (375°F) and fry the artichoke slices, a few at a time, for about 3 minutes or until crisp and golden. Drain them on kitchen paper and keep hot while you fry the rest. Serve at once sprinkled with salt.

Serves 8

Artichokes with Curry Sauce

0.5 kg (1 lb) Jerusalem
  artichokes, prepared
salt
250 ml (½ pint) béchamel
  sauce (see page 19)

30 ml (2 level tablespoons)
  mild curry powder
pepper

Cook the artichokes in plenty of boiling salted water until they are tender. Make the sauce, stir in the curry powder and check the seasoning. Drain the artichokes well, add them to the sauce and simmer vegetables and sauce together for 5 minutes. Turn into a hot dish to serve.

Serves 4

Spinach

1.5 kg (3 lb) spinach   freshly ground black
salt   pepper
50 g (2 oz) butter

Wash the spinach leaves in 2 or 3 changes of water, lifting each leaf separately to make sure all the grit has gone. Remove badly damaged leaves and thick stalks. Cook the spinach with just the water clinging to the leaves and some salt, covered, for about 10 minutes or until tender but not mushy. Transfer to a colander and run cold water over the leaves. Gently squeeze them as dry as possible. Return them to the pan and reheat them gently, turning them over and over to make sure they don't stick to the pan and burn. Add the butter, toss the leaves, and season well with plenty of freshly ground black pepper. Serve at once.

Serves 6

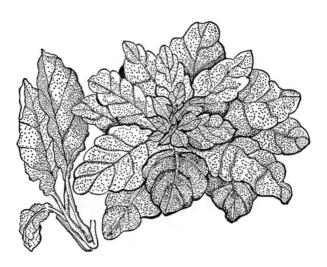

Spinach with Style

1.5 kg (3 lb) spinach,
  prepared
salt
4 rashers streaky bacon

Croûtons:
2 slices white bread

50 g (2 oz) butter
15 ml (1 tablespoon)
  cooking oil
1 clove garlic, finely
  chopped
pepper

Cook the spinach in plenty of fast-boiling salted water for 10 minutes or until the leaves are tender. Meanwhile, remove the bacon rinds, chop the rashers into tiny pieces and fry them with the bacon rinds until they are crisp. Drain well on kitchen paper.

To make the croûtons, remove the crusts from the bread and cut the slices into 1.25-cm (½-in) squares. Heat the butter in a frying pan with the oil, add the bread cubes and fry them, turning frequently, until crisp and golden on all sides. Add the garlic for the last minute of frying.

Drain the spinach and refresh it under cold water. Chop the leaves roughly and squeeze to remove as much water as possible. Reheat the spinach in a pan, being careful it doesn't catch on the bottom. Season with pepper. Then stir in the bacon pieces and the garlic croûtons.

Serves 6

Spinach Soufflé

250 ml (½ pint) béchamel
  sauce (see page 19)
0.75 kg (1½ lb) spinach,
  prepared
salt

25 g (1 oz) butter
4 large eggs, separated
pepper
15 ml (1 level tablespoon)
  Parmesan cheese, grated

Make the béchamel sauce and let it cool, pressing a wet piece of greaseproof paper on to the surface to prevent a skin forming. Cook the spinach in fast-boiling salted water for 10 minutes, then turn it into a colander and, when it has cooled a little, press out as much of the water as possible between the palms of your hands. Remove any remaining thick stems at this point. Chop the spinach finely, using a sharp knife. Put the spinach in a pan with the butter and stir it over a high heat to dry it. Remove the spinach from the heat and stir in the béchamel sauce and the egg yolks. Whisk well and season with salt and pepper. Whisk the egg whites until stiff, then fold them into the mixture and turn it at once into a buttered 15-cm (6-in) soufflé dish. Sprinkle with the cheese and bake at 190°C (375°F)/Gas 5 for about 45–50 minutes or until risen and golden. Serve at once.

Serves 4

New Potatoes

1 kg (2 lb) new potatoes
salt
50 g (2 oz) butter

15 ml (1 level tablespoon)
parsley, chopped

Scrub the potatoes to remove any loose skin and earth. There is no need to remove all the skin because it gives the cooked potatoes a delicious flavour, but if you want to remove it, scrape it off. Put the potatoes into salted water, bring to the boil and cook for 20 to 25 minutes until tender but not breaking. Drain well and serve with knobs of butter and sprinkled with the parsley.

Serves 6–8

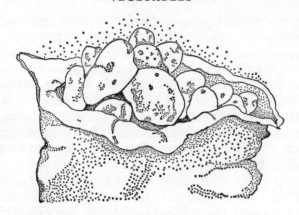

Sauté Potatoes

0.5 kg (1 lb) new potatoes,
   prepared
salt
50 g (2 oz) butter

15 ml (1 tablespoon)
   vegetable oil
5 ml (1 level teaspoon)
   chives, chopped
pepper

Boil the potatoes in salted water for 20 minutes or until they are just cooked but not really soft. Cut them into 0.5-cm (¼-in) slices. Heat the butter with the oil in a frying pan and add the potato slices. Fry them over a gentle heat, turning them once so that they are crisp and golden on both sides. Drain on kitchen paper and serve sprinkled with the chives and a little salt and pepper.

Serves 6

Baked New Potatoes

0.5 kg (1 lb) new potatoes,
   prepared
25 g (1 oz) butter

salt and pepper
sprigs of lemon thyme,
   mint and parsley

Choose even-sized potatoes for this dish for they are best left whole. Put the scrubbed potatoes in the centre of a square of thick foil. Dot with the butter and sprinkle with salt and freshly ground pepper. Add the sprigs of herbs and gather the foil corners to make a dolly-bag shape. Squeeze to seal. Put the bag on a baking tray and bake the potatoes at 200°C (400°F)/Gas 6 for about 1 hour. Squeeze the potatoes to see if they are cooked. Remove the herb sprigs and spoon the potatoes into a hot serving dish, pouring the melted butter over the top.

Serves 4

Boiled Courgettes

0.5 kg (1 lb) courgettes	5 ml (1 level teaspoon)
salt	parsley, finely chopped
pepper	

Top and tail the courgettes and cut them into 2.5-cm (1-in) lengths. Drop them into boiling salted water and simmer for 10 minutes or until they are soft but not squashy and still have a bite to them. Drain the courgettes well and serve them sprinkled with a little pepper and the parsley.

Serves 6

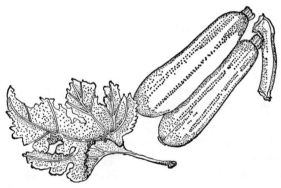

Courgettes Vinaigrette

0.5 kg (1 lb) courgettes,
 prepared
salt
vinaigrette (see page 46)

1 small onion, sliced
pepper
15 ml (1 level tablespoon)
 parsley, roughly chopped

Cut the courgettes into 2.5-cm (1-in) lengths and cook them
in boiling salted water for about 10 minutes or until tender
but not soft. Drain well and return the pan to the heat for a
minute or two to steam off extra liquid. Keep the courgette
pieces moving or they may stick to the saucepan and burn.
Turn the vegetables into a serving dish and pour on the
vinaigrette while they're still hot. Separate the onion slices
into rings. Sprinkle the courgettes with pepper and garnish
with onion rings and parsley.

Serves 4–6

Cheesy Baked Courgettes

0.75 kg (1½ lb) courgettes,
 sliced
1 clove garlic, crushed
60 ml (4 tablespoons) oil
2 medium-sized onions,
 sliced
salt and pepper

5 ml (1 level teaspoon)
 chives, chopped
142-g (5-oz) carton single
 cream
100 g (4 oz) Cheddar
 cheese, grated
4 large eggs, beaten

Put the courgettes and garlic with the oil in a frying pan and
stir them round together over a high heat until the courgettes
just begin to brown. Reduce the heat, add the onions, salt,
pepper and chives and cook slowly for 20 minutes or until
the onion is soft.

Stir the cream, grated cheese and beaten eggs together and
season this mixture with salt and pepper. Turn the vegetables
into an ovenproof dish, pour on the cheesy topping and bake
at 180°C (350°F)/Gas 4 for about 20 minutes or until the top
is set and golden brown.

Serves 4

Mange Tout with Herbs

0.75 kg (1½ lb) mange tout   5 ml (1 level teaspoon)
salt   chives, chopped
50 g (2 oz) butter   5 ml (1 level teaspoon)
pepper   lemon thyme, chopped

Mange tout are peas so tiny that they haven't begun to swell
the pod. You eat the whole tender – and delicious – pod.
Top and tail the mange tout and cook them in boiling salted
water for 5 minutes. Drain them well and return them to the
pan. Heat for 2 or 3 minutes to dry them, keeping them
moving in the pan so they don't stick and burn. Add the
butter and toss the mange tout to coat them well. Sprinkle on
pepper and the herbs and mix well again. Serve at once.

Serves 6

Mange Tout in Cream

0.5 kg (1 lb) mange tout, prepared
salt
25 g (1 oz) butter

125 ml (¼ pint) double cream
pepper
juice of ½ lemon, strained

Drop the mange tout into boiling salted water. Cook them for 5 minutes or until just tender. Drain well, using a colander. Melt the butter in the pan, add the mange tout and stir them around for 2 minutes to coat with butter. Pour in the cream and heat gently but do not let it boil. Season with pepper and some more salt if necessary. Serve sprinkled with the lemon juice.

Serves 6

Chinese Snow Peas

0.5 kg (1 lb) mange tout, prepared
30 ml (2 tablespoons) cooking oil
1 clove garlic, crushed

salt
45 ml (3 tablespoons) hot water
15 g (½ oz) lard

Dry the pods well after rinsing them because drops of water spit when they come in contact with the oil. Heat the oil in a heavy frying pan and add the mange tout. Stir them round over a gentle heat for about 1 minute. Remove from the heat and stir in the garlic, a sprinkling of salt and the hot water and stir-fry for another minute, lifting the peas carefully. Continue until most of the liquid has evaporated. Cut the lard into tiny pieces, add it to the pan and stir it over a low heat, turning the pods in the melted lard until each one glistens. Taste for seasoning, adding a little more salt if necessary, and serve at once.

Serves 4

Perfect French Beans

0.5 kg (1 lb) french beans	ground nutmeg
salt	knob of butter

Top and tail the beans but leave them whole. Drop them into boiling salted water and cook them for 15 to 20 minutes until tender. They shouldn't be soft enough to disintegrate when you eat them, but instead should have a slight bite. Drain them well and serve dusted with nutmeg and with a knob of butter sitting in the middle of the beans.

Serves 6

Beans à la Grèque

0.75 kg (1½ lb) french beans, prepared	1 clove garlic, crushed
salt	60 ml (4 tablespoons) olive oil
1 large onion, thinly sliced	pepper
6 large ripe tomatoes, sliced	30 ml (2 tablespoons) parsley, finely chopped

Cook the french beans in boiling salted water for 10 minutes, then drain them well. Put the onion, tomatoes and garlic in a frying pan with the olive oil and fry this mixture for 5 minutes. Stir in the beans and simmer for another 10 minutes until the beans are just cooked. Season well with salt and pepper, sprinkle with the parsley and serve hot or cold.

Serves 4

French Beans with Cheese Sauce

0.75 kg (1½ lb) french
   beans, prepared
salt

Cheese sauce:
25 g (1 oz) butter
25 g (1 oz) plain flour

250 ml (½ pint) milk
pepper
100 g (4 oz) Cheddar
   cheese, grated
ground nutmeg
25 g (1 oz) Parmesan
   cheese, grated

Cook the beans in boiling salted water for 15 minutes or until tender but not squashy.

Meanwhile, make a cheese sauce. Melt the butter in a saucepan, stir in the flour and cook for 1 minute. Remove from the heat and gradually stir in the milk. Bring to the boil, stirring all the time, and cook the sauce for 2 minutes, stirring frequently. Season well with salt and pepper and stir in 75 g (3 oz) Cheddar cheese and a good sprinkling of nutmeg.

Drain the beans well, stir them into the sauce and transfer to an ovenproof dish. Sprinkle with the remaining cheeses and place under a hot grill until the top is brown and bubbling.

Serves 6

Boiled Carrots

0.5 kg (1 lb) carrots
salt
15 g (½ oz) butter

pepper
15 ml (1 level tablespoon)
  parsley, chopped

Cut off the leaves and roots of the carrots and scrape them lightly with a sharp knife. Leave whole. Put into salted water and bring to the boil. Cook for 15 to 20 minutes until they are tender but not squashy. Drain well, then toss in the butter over a low heat. Sprinkle with pepper and the parsley and serve at once.

Serves 6

Glazed Carrots

50 g (2 oz) butter
0.5 kg (1 lb) carrots,
  prepared
15 ml (1 level tablespoon)
  caster sugar
salt

5 ml (1 teaspoon)
  lemon juice, strained
pepper
10 ml (1 level dessertspoon)
  parsley, chopped

Melt the butter in a saucepan, add the whole carrots, sugar, 3 ml ($\frac{1}{2}$ level teaspoon) salt and enough cold water to half cover the carrots. Bring to the boil, then cook gently without the lid, shaking the pan from time to time until the carrots are tender. The water should have completely evaporated by this time but if it hasn't, remove the carrots, keep them warm and boil the liquid in the pan until it is reduced to a glaze which is just enough to coat the carrots. Return the carrots to the pan. Add the lemon juice and pepper to taste and toss them to coat them in the glaze. Garnish with the parsley and serve at once.

Serves 6

Carrots with Cider

0.5 kg (1 lb) carrots, scraped
50 g (2 oz) butter
salt and pepper
60 ml (4 tablespoons) double cream
60 ml (4 tablespoons) cider
10 ml (2 teaspoons) lemon juice, strained
5 ml (1 level teaspoon) cornflour

Put the carrots, leaving them whole if small, in a pan with 25 g (1 oz) butter. Melt the butter and cook the carrots by shaking them in the butter until it has been absorbed. Keep the lid on the pan while you do this. Add boiling water to almost cover the carrots, season with salt and pepper and simmer them for about 15 minutes or until cooked but not breaking. Pour off any liquid that remains.

Melt the remaining butter in another pan and when it is hot, carefully stir in the cream, then gradually add the cider, stirring all the time. Finally add the lemon juice and season with salt and pepper. Mix the cornflour to a smooth paste with a little cold water, stir into the sauce and continue cooking and stirring until slightly thickened. Add the drained carrots and cook them very gently in this sauce for about 5 minutes until heated through.

Serves 4

Asparagus

0.5 kg (1 lb) asparagus	75 g (3 oz) unsalted butter,
salt	melted
pepper	

Wash the asparagus and trim the spears to the same length. Tie the spears in a bundle with thin white string. Bring 5 cm (2 in) salted water to the boil in a deep saucepan, deep enough to hold the asparagus upright with the lid on the pan. There are special asparagus cooking pans which hold the stalks upright, but these are expensive and I'm against pans with single uses. I've bought a cheap coffee percolator to use for asparagus. The glass dome provides an easy way to check on the cooking without having to lift the lid and lose the steam. If you buy a percolator, keep it specially for aspara-

gus. I know that makes it a one-use piece of equipment, but at least it won't cost a fortune. Drop the asparagus into the boiling water, stems first, and boil, covered, for about 12 minutes. The tender tips should steam rather than be boiled in water. Don't overcook asparagus because it should be tender but not so soft that you cannot pick it up with your fingers without it breaking. Drain well, lay the bundle on a plate and untie the string. Divide between the serving plates, sprinkle with pepper and pour melted butter over the spears.

Serves 6

Asparagus Flan

Shortcrust pastry:
200 g (8 oz) plain flour
salt
50 g (2 oz) margarine
50 g (2 oz) lard

225 g ($\frac{1}{2}$ lb) asparagus
2 large eggs
250 ml ($\frac{1}{2}$ pint) milk
30 ml (2 tablespoons)
    double cream
pepper

To make the shortcrust pastry, sift the flour and a pinch of salt into a bowl. Rub in the margarine and lard and mix to a stiff dough with cold water. Roll the pastry thinly and use to line a 20-cm (8-in) ovenproof pie dish, flan dish or flan ring standing on a baking tray.

Stand the asparagus in boiling salted water and cook, covered, for about 12 minutes. Make sure you trim off all woody stems after cooking so that every bit of remaining asparagus is edible. (Sprue – skinny spears – is often sold slightly cheaper than the fatter, more mature spears and is ideal for this recipe.)

Whisk the eggs, milk and double cream together and season with salt and pepper. Arrange the asparagus in the flan case, strain over the milk mixture and bake at 200°C (400°F)/Gas 6 for 30 to 35 minutes until the filling has set.

Serves 6

Asparagus Scramble

20 tiny asparagus tips	15 ml (1 tablespoon)
salt	double cream
50 g (2 oz) butter	30 ml (2 level tablespoons)
8 large eggs	Cheddar cheese, finely
pepper	grated

Use tiny asparagus tips for this dish, those that are too small to be served on a plate with a butter sauce. Drop them into gently boiling salted water and cook them until they are just tender. Drain them and keep them hot.

Melt the butter in a heavy saucepan. Whisk the eggs with salt and pepper and when the butter is foamy and beginning to turn brown, pour in the egg mixture. Stir with a wooden spoon until the eggs scramble, but stir in the cream, the cheese and the asparagus tips before it is cooked exactly as you like it. This dish should be creamy-looking, not dry. Serve with toast fingers or with cheese straws as a starter.

Serves 4

Spring Greens

0.5 kg (1 lb) spring greens	pepper
salt	

Wash the spring greens, discarding badly damaged leaves and cutting out any really thick stalks. Drop into fast-boiling salted water and cook for 10 minutes until tender. Drain well in a colander and using a saucer or small plate, press the greens to shape them into a flat cake and to get rid of more water. Divide the greens into portions and serve sprinkled with freshly ground black pepper.

Serves 6

Cabbage au Gratin

1 kg (2 lb) spring greens,
  prepared
salt
250 ml (½ pint) béchamel
  sauce (see page 19)

100 g (4 oz) Cheddar
  cheese, grated
pepper
50 g (2 oz) fresh white
  breadcrumbs

Cook the spring greens in plenty of boiling, salted water.
Drain well and chop finely, almost to a purée consistency.
Stir in the béchamel sauce and half the grated cheese. Check
the seasoning, adding more if necessary. Turn this mixture
into a fireproof dish. Mix the remaining cheese with the
breadcrumbs and sprinkle all over the greens. Place under a
hot grill until the cheese topping is golden brown.

Serves 8

Stuffed Cabbage Rolls

16 large cabbage leaves
1 medium-sized onion,
   chopped
50 g (2 oz) long-grain rice,
   cooked
25 g (1 oz) butter
300 g (12 oz) fresh lamb,
   minced

salt and pepper
5 ml (1 level teaspoon)
   ground coriander
5 ml (1 level teaspoon)
   lemon rind, finely grated
500 ml (1 pint) good
   chicken stock

Use only the best and largest leaves from a cabbage for the rolls. Put the leaves in a large bowl and pour on boiling water. Leave while you make the filling. Fry the onion and rice in the butter for about 5 minutes then add the meat, salt and pepper, coriander and lemon rind. Mix well and moisten with 250 ml ($\frac{1}{2}$ pint) stock. Cook, covered, for 10 minutes.

Remove the cabbage leaves, which should be limp enough to roll, from the water. Remove any thick stalks and divide the filling mixture between the leaves, putting it towards the stalk ends. Roll from the stalks, folding in the sides.

Arrange the rolls in an ovenproof dish, packing them tightly together so they don't unroll in the cooking. Pour on the remaining stock, cover with foil and bake them at 160°C (325°F)/Gas 3 for 1 to 1$\frac{1}{2}$ hours. Serve the rolls with a little of the stock as a gravy.

Serves 4

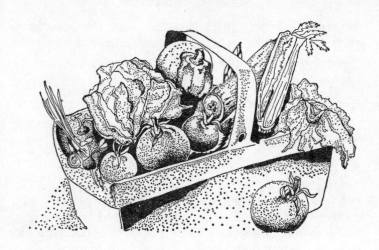

Salads

Traditionally, the British have always been weak on salads due, largely, to the lack of many sunny days. When recently we had two long hot summers in a row, most of us began to be bored with the usual variety of salads. With the hope that our summer weather really is getting warmer, look again at your salad ideas. Some of the recipes in this chapter are favourites, but a few may be new to you and I've also included some nice dressings which can give new flavours to your own salad preferences.

Green Salad

1 lettuce, prepared
1 bunch watercress,
   prepared

3 sticks celery, sliced
¼ cucumber, thinly sliced
vinaigrette (see page 46)

Arrange the best lettuce leaves around a serving bowl. Cut

the remainder into strips and mix with the watercress, celery and cucumber. Toss in the vinaigrette. Arrange in the centre of the lettuce leaves.

Serves 6

Rice Salad

450 g (1 lb) long-grain
    rice, cooked
1 large green eating apple,
    chopped
1 large onion, chopped
100 g (4 oz) mixed chopped
    nuts, toasted

1 large green pepper,
    chopped
salt and pepper
90 ml (6 level tablespoons)
    mayonnaise (see page 46)
100 g (4 oz) button
    mushrooms, sliced

Mix the rice with the apple, onion, nuts and green pepper and season well with salt and pepper. Stir in the mayonnaise well, then gently stir in the raw mushrooms.

Serves 8

Waldorf Salad

4 sticks celery, diced
3 red eating apples, diced
45 ml (3 level tablespoons)
    mayonnaise (see page 46)

1 small lettuce, prepared
75 g (3 oz) walnuts,
    chopped

Mix the celery and apple with the mayonnaise. Arrange the lettuce leaves on a serving plate. Mix the nuts into the salad and pile on to the lettuce leaves. Serve at once.

Serves 8

Cucumber Salad

1 large cucumber, peeled   30 ml (2 level tablespoons)
salt   soured cream
vinaigrette (see page 46)   15 ml (1 level tablespoon)
                                          parsley, chopped

Thinly slice the cucumber and put it in a basin, sprinkling
each layer liberally with salt. Leave to stand for at least 1
hour. Turn the cucumber into a colander and rinse well
under running cold water. Taste to make sure that the salt
has been rinsed away. Drain well, toss in vinaigrette and put
into a serving dish. Spoon the soured cream into the centre
and sprinkle with the parsley.

Serves 4–6

Coleslaw

1 medium-sized white   juice of 1 lemon, strained
  cabbage, finely shredded   100 g (4 oz) sultanas
1 medium-sized onion,   90 ml (6 level tablespoons)
  chopped   mayonnaise (see page 46)
1 large eating apple,   salt and pepper
  chopped

Mix the cabbage with the onion. Toss the apple in lemon
juice as soon as you have chopped it to prevent it going
brown. Add to the cabbage with the sultanas. Mix in the
mayonnaise and season well with salt and pepper.

Serves 8

Potato Salad

0.5 kg (1 lb) large new
   potatoes, prepared
salt
30 ml (2 tablespoons)
   vinaigrette (see page 46)

45 ml (3 level tablespoons)
   blender mayonnaise
   (see page 47)
15 ml (1 level tablespoon)
   parsley, chopped

Cook the potatoes, in their skins, in plenty of boiling salted water for about 20 minutes or until just cooked. Remove the skins while still hot and cut the potatoes into dice. Pour over the vinaigrette and leave to cool completely. Mix with the mayonnaise and parsley and serve.

Serves 6

Spinach Salad

0.5 kg (1 lb) spinach
60 ml (4 level tablespoons)
   blender mayonnaise (see
   page 47)

1 large egg, hard-boiled

Use only the youngest, most tender spinach leaves for a salad and wash them in plenty of cold water, changing the water several times to make sure you get rid of all the grit. Shred the leaves and stir them lightly into the mayonnaise. Chop the egg and use to garnish the salad.

Serves 4

Mediterranean Beans

0.5 kg (1 lb) french beans,
   prepared
salt
20 black olives

75 g (3 oz) Greek feta
   cheese, blue cheese or
   Wensleydale
vinaigrette (see page 46)

Cook the beans in boiling salted water until they are just
tender. Drain well and cut them into short lengths. Mix with
the olives. Cut the cheese into small pieces, about the size of
the olives, and stir them gently into the salad with the
vinaigrette.

Serves 4

Banana, Raisin and Carrot Salad

4 large carrots, finely
  grated
8 large bananas, thinly
  sliced
100 g (4 oz) seedless raisins
50 g (2 oz) almonds,
  chopped
vinaigrette (see page 46)

Mix the carrots, bananas, raisins (use sultanas if you have no
seedless raisins) and almonds with the vinaigrette in a
serving bowl.

Serves 8

Beetroot Salad

4 large beetroot, cooked
1 small onion, finely
  chopped
vinaigrette (see page 46)
5 ml (1 level teaspoon)
  horseradish, freshly
  grated

It's best to cook the beetroot yourself. Greengrocers tend to
cook it until it is a little too soft; for my taste, it's better with
a bite to it. Slice the beetroot, not too thinly, and arrange it
on a serving dish. Sprinkle with the onion and vinaigrette
and grate a little horseradish on top to serve.

Serves 8

Onion and Mint Salad

1 bunch of spring onions,
  prepared
2 or 3 large sprigs of mint,
  finely chopped

5 ml (1 level teaspoon)
  caster sugar
yoghurt dressing (see page
  48)

Cut the onions into thin slices and arrange them on a serving plate. Sprinkle with the mint and the caster sugar. Pour on the yoghurt dressing and allow to stand for 30 minutes before you serve.

Serves 4

Two-tone Salad

1 lettuce
1 bunch mustard and cress

creamy garlic sauce (see
  page 48)
1 large egg, hard-boiled

Cut off the root of the lettuce and discard any damaged outer leaves and those that are really coarse. Separate the remaining leaves and wash them under running cold water. Cut off the roots of the mustard and cress, pick it over, removing dead leaves, and rinse in a sieve under running cold water. Dry both ingredients well and mix them in a serving bowl. Pour on the garlic sauce, toss gently to coat well and serve garnished with the chopped egg.

Serves 6

Crudité with Sauce Verte

½ cucumber, peeled
4 carrots, scraped
8 radishes, prepared

8 spring onions, prepared
sauce verte (see page 47)

Cut the cucumber into long thin strips, then cut these strips in half across. Cut the carrots into similar sizes. Arrange the cucumber, carrots, radishes and spring onions attractively on a round plate, putting a small bowl in the centre. Spoon the sauce verte into the bowl and serve as a first course or as a nibble before dinner.

Serves 4–6

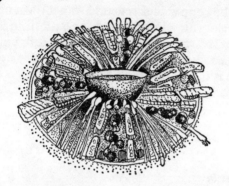

Potato and Radish Dip

0.5 kg (1 lb) very small   1 large bunch radishes,
   new potatoes, prepared   prepared
salt   aïoli (see page 47)

Ideally, the potatoes should be the same size as the radishes and as there's no need to peel the potatoes, it's not too arduous to prepare the tiny ones for this dish. Cook the scrubbed potatoes in boiling salted water until just tender but not breaking up. Drain them well and allow to cool. Mix the potatoes and radishes together and stir in 15 ml (1 tablespoon) of the aïoli to coat them. Spoon them on to a serving dish and transfer the rest of the aïoli to a small dish. Serve with cocktail sticks, or divide them on to individual plates with some sauce if they form part of a main course salad.

Serves 6

Vinaigrette

good pinch of salt
good pinch of pepper
3 ml ($\frac{1}{2}$ level teaspoon)
  mustard powder

60 ml (4 tablespoons)
  vinegar
125 ml ($\frac{1}{4}$ pint) olive oil

Put the salt, pepper and mustard in a bowl and mix to a smooth paste with a little of the vinegar. Stir in the remaining vinegar and the oil and whisk with a fork until the mixture thickens slightly. Pour at once over a salad, or if the vinaigrette is to be served in a jug, whisk it again just before using it at table.

Serves 8

Mayonnaise

1 large egg yolk
pinch of mustard powder
pinch of salt
pinch of pepper
125 ml ($\frac{1}{4}$ pint) olive oil

15 ml (1 tablespoon) white
  wine vinegar
10 ml (1 dessertspoon)
  lemon juice, strained

Put the egg yolk in a basin. Add the mustard, salt and pepper and, using a wooden spoon, beat the egg yolk well. Begin to add the oil, a drop at a time, beating well after each addition. Don't add the next drop until the last one has been beaten in; too much oil at this stage can result in a curdled mixture. If it looks as though it might curdle, stop adding oil and beat well. Continue adding oil a little more quickly after half the amount has been beaten in. Beat in the vinegar and lemon juice, check seasoning and add more if required.

   Should your mayonnaise curdle at any time during the mixing, and beating hard won't correct it, break a fresh egg yolk into a clean bowl, then gradually and slowly beat in the curdled mixture. Finally you may add the remaining olive oil.

Serves 4–6

Blender Mayonnaise

1 large egg
30 ml (2 tablespoons)
   lemon juice or vinegar
3 ml (½ level teaspoon) salt
3 ml (½ level teaspoon)
   pepper

good pinch of mustard
   powder
125 ml (¼ pint) vegetable
   oil

Put the egg, lemon juice or vinegar and seasonings in a blender. Begin to blend and add the oil in a steady stream through the hole in the lid. This should take 1 minute and make perfect mayonnaise every time.

Serves 4–6

Aïoli

2 large cloves garlic,
   crushed

125 ml (¼ pint) mayonnaise
   (see page 46)

Make the mayonnaise in the usual way, adding the crushed garlic cloves with the other seasonings to the egg yolk.

Serves 4–6

Sauce Verte

12 sprigs of watercress
12 sprigs of parsley
6 leaves of spinach

6 leaves of tarragon
125 ml (¼ pint) mayonnaise
   (see page 46)

Blanch the watercress, parsley, spinach and tarragon leaves in fast-boiling water for about 2 minutes. Strain the leaves, squeeze them dry, then pound them to a purée with the end of a wooden rolling pin. Stir this mixture into the mayonnaise. It should colour as well as flavour.

Serves 4–6

Creamy Garlic Sauce

good pinch of caster sugar
45 ml (3 tablespoons) warm water
5 ml (1 level teaspoon) Dijon mustard
30 ml (2 tablespoons) salad oil

15 ml (1 tablespoon) white vinegar
salt and pepper
1 clove garlic, crushed
90 ml (6 tablespoons) double cream

Dissolve the sugar in the water. Stir in the mustard, then whisk in the oil, vinegar and salt and pepper. Whisk in the crushed garlic and double cream. Check the seasoning and serve.

Serves 4–6

Yoghurt Dressing

30 ml (2 level tablespoons) chives, chopped
10 ml (1 level dessertspoon) English mustard

15 ml (1 tablespoon) lemon juice, strained
salt and pepper
2 142-g (5-oz) cartons natural yoghurt

Stir the chives, mustard, lemon juice and salt and pepper to taste into the yoghurt. Whisk well and serve.

Serves 8

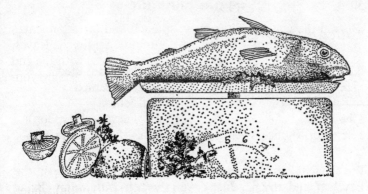

Fish

Mackerel, skate, lemon sole and turbot are about now and make welcome changes of flavour from the haddock, herring and whiting of earlier in the year. Brill, bass, whitebait and grey mullet can be found as well, though not in such plentiful supply, mainly because we don't know what to do with them. Generally plenty are caught but we British are conservative – much to the despair of at least one fishmonger, my own, who wins prizes for his displays and varieties of fish but sells mostly cod fillets.

Whitebait is a great delicacy, expensive in restaurants but not ruinous if you cook your own. Usually whitebait are the fry (or little ones) of the herring and sprat. After washing them well, but carefully because they are delicate, fry them whole. Brill, a much underrated fish, makes wonderful soufflés, light and delicate, and provides a chance to show off your mousseline sauce. Cockles are in season and can be added to pies in place of mussels or fried with bacon as a breakfast or snack. But for the true cockle-lover, nothing will persuade him that cockles soused in vinegar are anything but the best. There are recipes here, too, for cod and coley, year-round favourites made into fish cakes, a mousseline, curry dishes, and a fish crumble.

Potted Mackerel

0.75 kg (1½ lb) mackerel,
  filleted
salt and pepper
1 bay leaf
1 sprig of thyme

100 g (4 oz) unsalted
  butter, creamed
1 small lemon
15 ml (1 level tablespoon)
  chives, finely chopped

Put the mackerel in a pan and season it with salt, pepper, the bay leaf and thyme. Just cover the fish with water. Bring gently to the boil, reduce the heat to the lowest simmer and cook the fish for 10 minutes. Drain and reserve the fish liquid. Remove any skin and bones from the fillets and blend until smooth with 45–60 ml (3–4 tablespoons) fish liquid. Gradually beat the smooth fish mixture into the creamed butter. Finely grate the rind of the lemon and squeeze and strain the juice. Add rind, juice and chives to the mackerel. Check seasoning, adding more salt and freshly ground pepper if required. Spoon into 6 individual serving dishes or into a small bowl and smooth. Chill until firm, then serve with toast or thin brown bread and butter.

If you wish to keep this potted mackerel for a few days before serving it, melt another 50 g (2 oz) butter but don't let it bubble or brown. Stir in some more chopped chives – about 5 ml (1 level teaspoon) – and pour this mixture over the fish. Allow to set.

Serves 6

Deep-fried Whitebait

0.5 kg (1 lb) whitebait
45 ml (3 level tablespoons)
  plain flour
salt and pepper

oil for deep frying
sprigs of parsley
cayenne pepper
lemon wedges

Rinse the whitebait carefully, drain well and dry completely with kitchen paper. Mix the flour with a good pinch each of salt and pepper and toss the fish in this until they are well coated. Heat the oil to 182°C (360°F) or until a 2.5-cm (1-in) cube of bread browns in 60 seconds. Fry the whitebait in 4 batches for 2 to 3 minutes each batch. Drain on kitchen paper and keep hot while you fry the remainder. Serve garnished with parsley, cayenne pepper and lemon wedges.

Serves 4

Fish Cakes

0.75 kg (1½ lb) coley
salt
pepper
0.75 kg (1½ lb) potatoes,
  mashed
75 g (3 oz) butter

30 ml (2 level tablespoons)
  parsley, chopped
2 large eggs, beaten
100 g (4 oz) fresh white
  breadcrumbs
50 g (2 oz) lard

Put the fish in a pan with a good pinch of salt and cover with cold water. Bring to the boil and simmer for about 10 minutes. Drain and flake the fish, removing skin and bones. Season with salt and pepper and mix with the potatoes, butter and parsley. Stir in enough beaten egg to mix. Flouring your hands each time, form the fish mixture into round cakes each about 2.5 cm (1 in) thick. Coat each cake with the remaining egg and the breadcrumbs, patting them on well. Fry in the lard until golden brown on both sides. Drain well and serve with tomato ketchup.

Serves 8

Mackerel with Gooseberry Sauce

4 medium-sized mackerel,
   cleaned
salt and pepper
15 ml (1 tablespoon)
   cooking oil

Gooseberry sauce:
350 g (12 oz) gooseberries,
   prepared
50 g (2 oz) granulated
   sugar
10 ml (1 level dessertspoon)
   arrowroot
1 large lemon

Rinse the mackerel, pat dry, then season the insides with salt and pepper. Brush with half the oil and arrange on a grill pan. Cook under a hot grill for 7 to 8 minutes on each side, using the remaining oil to brush the mackerel when you turn them over.

Meanwhile, put the gooseberries in a saucepan with 125 ml (¼ pint) cold water and the sugar. Cook until the gooseberries are soft but not breaking. Blend the arrowroot with a little cold water, pour on some of the gooseberry juice, then return this mixture to the saucepan. Bring to the boil, stirring all the time until the sauce has thickened and cleared. Finely grate the rind from the lemon and squeeze and strain the juice. Stir rind and juice into the sauce. Check that it's sweet enough for your liking and stir in more sugar if necessary. Serve the sauce with the grilled mackerel.

Serves 4

Russian Cod Pie

350 g ($\frac{3}{4}$ lb) cod fillet
salt
214-g (7$\frac{1}{2}$-oz) packet
   frozen puff pastry,
   thawed

Parsley velouté sauce:
40 g (1$\frac{1}{2}$ oz) butter
40 g (1$\frac{1}{2}$ oz) plain flour
250 ml ($\frac{1}{2}$ pint) fish liquid
125 ml ($\frac{1}{4}$ pint) milk
60 ml (4 level tablespoons)
   parsley, chopped
pepper
2 large eggs, hard-boiled

Put the cod in a pan of cold water and add a good pinch of salt. Bring to the boil, then simmer for about 10 minutes. Drain, reserving 250 ml ($\frac{1}{2}$ pint) fish liquid for the sauce, then flake the fish, removing skin and bones. Roll the pastry thinly to a large square and place it on a baking tray. Trim the edges.

For the sauce, melt the butter in a pan, stir in the flour and cook for 1 minute. Remove from the heat and gradually stir in the reserved fish liquid and the milk. Bring to the boil, stirring all the time, then cook the sauce for 2 minutes. Stir in the parsley and season to taste with salt and pepper. Mix half the sauce with the fish and put this in the centre of the pastry square. Keep the remaining sauce from forming a skin by wetting a piece of greaseproof paper and pressing it on the sauce's surface. Chop the eggs and put them on top of the fish. Brush the edges of the pastry with water and gather the 4 corners to the centre to form an envelope shape. Press the edges well to seal. Bake at 220°C (425°F)/Gas 7 for 30 minutes or until the pastry is golden and well risen. Serve with the remainder of the parsley sauce.

Serves 6

Turbot with Mousseline Sauce

½ small onion, finely
  chopped
4 medium-sized turbot
  steaks
rind of 1 lemon
few parsley stalks
30 ml (2 tablespoons)
  white wine (optional)
salt and pepper

Mousseline sauce:
2 large egg yolks
10 ml (1 dessertspoon)
  warm water
100 g (4 oz) unsalted
  butter, softened
salt and pepper
10 ml (2 teaspoons) lemon
  juice, strained
30 ml (2 tablespoons)
  double cream, whipped

Put the onion in a pan large enough to hold the fish steaks in one layer. Wipe the fish and add to the pan with the lemon rind, parsley stalks, wine and a pinch of salt and pepper. Add cold water to just cover the fish. Cover with a lid and bring slowly to the boil. Reduce the heat and poach the fish gently for 15 minutes.

Meanwhile, make the mousseline sauce. Whisk the egg yolks and warm water together in the top of a double saucepan or in a basin standing over a pan of very hot water. This sauce must not boil. Very gradually add the softened butter, whisking all the time. When the butter has been incorporated, season the sauce carefully with salt and pepper and the lemon juice. Then gently whisk in the whipped cream and be ready to serve the sauce at once.

Carefully lift the fish from the pan and drain it very well, then put each steak on a warm plate. Spoon on the mousseline sauce to partly cover the fish at one side and serve immediately with boiled potatoes.

Serves 4

Florentine Brill

1 kg (2 lb) brill fillets	250 ml (½ pint) béchamel
sprig of thyme	sauce (see page 19)
6 peppercorns	60 ml (4 tablespoons)
piece of lemon rind	double cream
1 kg (2 lb) spinach,	75 g (3 oz) Gruyère or
prepared	Cheddar cheese, grated
salt	ground nutmeg

Rinse the fish fillets, fold them in three and arrange them in a large pan with the thyme, peppercorns and lemon rind. Add enough cold water to just cover the fish, bring it slowly to the boil, then reduce the heat and simmer the fillets for 10 minutes or until just cooked but not breaking up.

While the fish cooks, wash the spinach and pack the leaves into a saucepan with no other liquid than the water clinging to them. Add a sprinkle of salt and bring slowly to the boil and cook for 10 minutes or until tender. Make the béchamel sauce as directed on page 19.

Drain the fish carefully. Drain the spinach, pressing to remove all the water. Put the spinach in a 1-litre (2-pint) ovenproof dish and arrange the fish fillets on top. Stir the cream into the sauce with the grated cheese (use Cheddar if preferred, because Gruyère is very expensive these days) and add a dash of nutmeg. Spoon the sauce over the fish to cover completely and bake at 200°C (400°F)/Gas 6 for 10 minutes until browning nicely on top.

Serves 6

Mousseline of Fish

1 kg (2 lb) coley fillets	salt and pepper
4 large egg whites, lightly beaten	500 ml (1 pint) velouté sauce (see page 53)
250 ml (½ pint) double cream	4 large eggs, hard-boiled

Skin the coley fillets and blend the fish (cut into small pieces) with the egg whites and double cream until you have a smooth purée. Season the mixture with salt and pepper and turn it into a well-buttered soufflé dish or basin and cover the top with greaseproof paper. Steam the mousseline for about 40 minutes or until it is firm to the touch. Leave it for a couple of minutes before turning it out, or serve it straight from an attractive dish. Make the sauce as directed on page 53, but without the parsley. Chop the eggs, add to the sauce and pour it over the mousseline.

This is also good cold with mayonnaise.

Serves 8

Turbot with Shrimp Sauce

4 turbot steaks	25 g (1 oz) plain flour
1 large lemon, sliced	250 ml (½ pint) milk
salt and pepper	125 ml (¼ pint) fish liquid
	salt and pepper
Shrimp sauce:	175 g (6 oz) shrimps,
25 g (1 oz) butter	peeled

Arrange the turbot steaks in a well-buttered ovenproof dish. Cover with the lemon slices, sprinkle with salt and pepper and add 125 ml (¼ pint) cold water. Cook the fish in the oven at 180°C (350°F)/Gas 4 for about 15–20 minutes.

Melt the butter in a pan, stir in the flour and cook for 1 minute. Remove from the heat and gradually stir in the milk. Lift the fish carefully from the dish and arrange on serving plates. Strain the fish liquid and add it gradually to the sauce, stirring all the time. Bring to the boil and simmer the sauce for 2 minutes. Season well with salt and pepper (but go easy on the salt until you taste it after the shrimps have been added). Stir in the shrimps and allow to heat through for 2 minutes. Taste the sauce, add more seasoning if necessary and pour it over the turbot.

Serves 4

Brill with Onion Sauce

1 kg (2 lb) brill fillets	25 g (1 oz) plain flour
15 ml (1 tablespoon) lemon juice, strained	90 ml (6 tablespoons) fish liquid
salt and pepper	142-g (5-oz) carton single cream
Onion sauce:	salt and pepper
100 g (4 oz) onions, sliced	5 ml (1 level teaspoon) made mustard
25 g (1 oz) butter	

Skin the brill fillets and fold each one in three. Arrange them in a well-buttered ovenproof dish. Pour on the lemon juice and 90 ml (6 tablespoons) water. Season with salt and pepper. Cover the fish with a butter paper and cook it in the oven at 180°C (350°F)/Gas 4 for about 10 minutes.

Meanwhile, cook the onions in the butter in a heavy saucepan over a medium heat for 10 minutes. Stir in the flour and cook this mixture for 1 minute, stirring occasionally. Remove the fillets from the dish and keep them warm. Gradually add the fish liquid to the pan, stirring all the time, then stir in the cream. Season the sauce with salt and pepper, bring it to the boil and cook it gently for 2 minutes, stirring occasionally. Stir in the mustard, check the sauce for seasoning and pour it over the fillets. Serve at once.

Serves 6

Sole in Cider

1 kg (2 lb) lemon sole
  fillets
250 ml (½ pint) dry cider

Cider sauce:
25 g (1 oz) butter
25 g (1 oz) plain flour
250 ml (½ pint) cider liquid

15 ml (1 tablespoon) lemon
  juice, strained
15 ml (1 level tablespoon)
  parsley, finely chopped
60 ml (4 tablespoons)
  single cream
salt and pepper

Skin the fillets, removing the dark skin and the white skin
if you wish. Fold the fillets in three with the white skin, if
you've left it on, inside. Arrange them in a buttered
ovenproof dish and pour on the cider and 60 ml (4 tablespoons) cold water. Cover with a butter paper. Cook the
fish in the oven at 180°C (350°F)/Gas 4 for 15–20 minutes.

Meanwhile, melt the butter in a pan, stir in the flour and
cook this mixture for 1 minute. Remove the sauce from the
heat while you lift the fish from the liquid, arrange it on a
serving dish and strain the liquid. Gradually add the cider
liquid to the pan, stirring all the time, then bring the sauce
to the boil, stirring, and cook it gently for 2 minutes. Stir
in the lemon juice, parsley, cream and seasoning and pour
the sauce over the fish.

Serves 6

Fish Crumble

0.75 kg (1½ lb) cod
15 ml (1 level tablespoon)
  plain flour
salt and pepper
60 ml (4 tablespoons) top
  of the milk
225 g (½ lb) tomatoes,
  thinly sliced

225 g (8 oz) porridge oats
100 g (4 oz) butter, melted
5 ml (1 level teaspoon)
  mixed dried herbs
50 g (2 oz) Cheddar
  cheese, grated

Skin the fish and cut it into small chunks. Season the flour with salt and pepper and coat the fish with this. Put the fish with all the seasoned flour in an ovenproof dish. Pour on the top of the milk and cover the fish with the tomato slices.

Put the oats in a bowl and mix with the melted butter. Then stir in the herbs and press this mixture over the fish. Bake at 190°C (375°F)/Gas 5 for 30 minutes or until the crumble is beginning to turn brown. Sprinkle the cheese on the top and bake for another 10 minutes.

Serves 8

Baked Bass with Mushrooms

1 kg (2 lb) bass fillets
100 g (4 oz) button
  mushrooms, sliced
30 ml (2 tablespoons)
  white wine

salt and pepper
375 ml ($\frac{3}{4}$ pint) parsley
  velouté sauce (see page
  53)

Skin the fillets and arrange them in an ovenproof dish, one in which they may be served. Sprinkle them with the mushrooms, pour on the wine and 125 ml ($\frac{1}{4}$ pint) cold water and season with salt and pepper. Cover the dish with a butter paper and bake the fish in the oven at 180°C (350°F)/ Gas 4 for 15 minutes.

Meanwhile make the sauce as directed on page 53, making the fish liquid from this dish up to 250 ml ($\frac{1}{2}$ pint) with cold water if necessary. Season it carefully and pour it over the fish before serving.

Serves 8

Skate in Black Butter

2 wings of skate weighing
  0.75 kg (1½ lb) together
1 carrot, sliced
1 onion, halved
2 cloves
6 peppercorns
30 ml (2 tablespoons)
  vinegar
250 ml (¼ pint) cold water

1 bay leaf
1 sprig of thyme
75 g (3 oz) butter
60 ml (4 tablespoons) white
  wine vinegar
15 ml (1 level tablespoon)
  capers
15 ml (1 level tablespoon)
  parsley, finely chopped

Cut the skate wings into wedges. Put the carrot, onion, cloves, peppercorns, ordinary vinegar, water, bay leaf and thyme in a deep frying pan and boil for 15 minutes. Add the fish and bring slowly to the boil again. Simmer gently for 15 to 20 minutes. Lift out the fish, drain on kitchen paper and scrape off any skin. Arrange the pieces on a serving dish and keep hot. Discard the liquid and heat the pan. Add the butter and fry it to a rich brown colour. Although it's called black butter, it never is. Spoon it over the fish and again keep hot. Add the white wine vinegar to the pan, boil to reduce by half and pour over the fish. Sprinkle with the capers and parsley and serve at once with plain boiled potatoes.

Serves 6

Cockles and Bacon

72 large cockles
6 rashers streaky bacon,
  chopped

4 slices of bread
25 g (1 oz) butter

If you ever gather cockles yourself from the seashore, pick only those that are about 5 cm (2 in) across the shell; smaller ones are more trouble than they're worth. Wash them first to remove any sand. Soak them overnight in a bucket of clean water. Next day, bring a large pan of water to the boil.

Check each cockle for signs of life (like mussels, if they're alive they should be closed tight or they'll certainly snap to if you tap them), discarding any that are obviously dead. Drop them one at a time into the boiling water and cook them for about 5 minutes. By this time they should have opened and can be removed from the shells. Discard any that haven't opened during cooking. If you can get cockles from your fishmonger, he will have cooked them to this stage for you.

Fry the bacon in its own fat until it is crisp. Remove from the pan, leaving all the fat behind, then add the cockles and fry them in bacon fat for a few minutes. Toast and butter the bread, mix the bacon with the cockles and pile the mixture on the toast.

Serves 4

Grilled Mullet

4 grey mullet, cleaned	salt
few parsley stalks	100 g (4 oz) butter, softened
1 bay leaf	1 sprig of mint, finely
1 lemon	chopped
1 small onion, chopped	3 sprigs of thyme, finely
6 peppercorns	chopped
90 ml (6 tablespoons) oil	pepper
90 ml (6 tablespoons) vinegar	

Rinse the fish and pat them dry with kitchen paper. Put them in a dish long enough and wide enough to take the fish in one layer. Arrange the parsley stalks and bay leaf on the fish. Pare off all the lemon rind and add it to the dish with the onion, peppercorns, oil and vinegar. Sprinkle with salt and leave them to marinate for a couple of hours, turning them occasionally. Remove from the marinade and grill the fish on a greased grid under a medium heat for about 10 minutes, turning them once and basting them frequently with the marinade.

Meanwhile, squeeze and strain the lemon juice. Beat it gradually into the butter with the mint and thyme and some pepper. Serve with the fish. If you make this half an hour ahead of the cooking, return the butter to the fridge to become firm again.

Serves 4

Curried Cod

0.75 kg (1½ lb) cod fillet
1 large onion, chopped
25 g (1 oz) butter
15 ml (1 level tablespoon)
  curry powder
1 chicken stock cube

125 ml (¼ pint) boiling
  water
50 g (2 oz) sultanas
198-g (7-oz) can pineapple
  tidbits
salt and pepper

Wash the fish and cut it into 5-cm (2-in) pieces. Put the onion and butter in a frying pan and fry gently for 5 minutes. Stir in the curry powder. Dissolve the stock cube in the boiling water and add it to the pan. Bring to the boil, then add the sultanas and pineapple pieces and half the pineapple juice. Simmer for 10 minutes. Now add the fish pieces and simmer for 10 minutes more or until the fish is cooked. Season if necessary with salt and pepper. Serve with plain boiled rice.

Serves 6

Cod and Cockle Pie

100 g (4 oz) onion,
  chopped
100 g (4 oz) carrot,
  chopped
50 g (2 oz) butter
few parsley stalks
2 sprigs of thyme
0.5 kg (1 lb) cod
12 cockles (prepared, see
  page 60)

425-g (15-oz) can
  tomatoes
salt and pepper
213-g (7½-oz) packet
  frozen puff pastry,
  thawed
little egg (beaten) or milk

Put the onion and carrot in a saucepan with the butter, parsley stalks and thyme and fry them for 20 minutes, covered, over a gentle heat until the carrot is tender. Cut the cod into 5-cm (2-in) cubes, removing the skin and bones in the process. Add the cod to the pan with the cockles (if they're not already cooked) and the tomatoes. Break the tomatoes down a little with a wooden spoon. Season well with salt and pepper and simmer for about 10 minutes. Transfer the contents to an ovenproof pie dish. (If your cockles are from the fishmonger and cooked, add them at this stage of the recipe.)

Roll the pastry on a lightly-floured board to a 0.5-cm (¼-in) thickness and cut out rounds using a 7-cm (3-in) fluted cutter. Overlap the rounds all over the dish. Brush them with a little beaten egg or milk and bake at 230°C (450°F)/Gas 8 for about 30 minutes or until the pastry is golden brown and well puffed.

Serves 8

Meat

Thankfully the butchers' stock is year-round, consistently good and, I think, not expensive if one compares a pound of mince with a packet of cigarettes. Pork and beef don't have their seasons and it's too soon for home-produced veal, but the new season's lamb is arriving and sweet it tastes, too. You'll also find the baby chickens called poussins. There is a 'single' size weighing about 450 g (1 lb) and a 'double' which weighs roughly twice as much. 'Singles' are just right for one person and 'doubles' for two.

Ducklings are also available. These weigh about 1.35–1.5 kg (3–3½ lb); don't buy them any smaller for the proportion of bone to meat will be too great. Ducklings have less meat on them than chickens and you must allow about 450 g (1 lb) dressed weight per person when calculating for your recipes, whereas a chicken weighing 1.35 kg (3 lb) will serve four people. Nowadays there are so many battery-raised, oven-ready chickens about that I think another generation will not know the true taste of a chicken that has been scratching about, getting muscles on its legs perhaps, but developing a far better taste in so doing. When you do manage to find a free-range bird, roast it simply with lemon for flavouring and butter to supply the fat for cooking.

In this chapter there are all kinds of good ways to serve lamb, chicken and duck plus some suggestions for making pâté, terrine and mousse dishes and for enclosing meats in pastry for special occasions. And for lovers of the Chinese sweet and sour, there's a recipe for chicken in this sauce cooked by the very quick stir-fry method.

Roast Poussins

4 poussins (single size)   4 sprigs of thyme
salt and pepper   50 g (2 oz) butter

Wipe the tiny chickens inside and out. Sprinkle inside and out with salt and pepper and put a sprig of thyme inside each bird. Arrange the birds in a roasting dish, dot with the butter and roast for about 20 minutes at 200°C (400°F)/Gas 6 or until they are golden brown and the skin is crisp. Serve one to each person just as they are or if liked with a good chicken gravy.

Serves 4

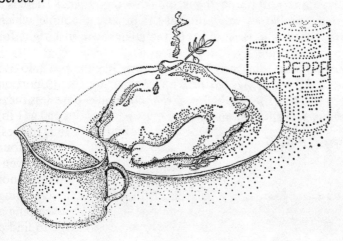

Lamb en Croûte

1.5 kg (3 lb) shank end of
  lamb, boned
2 lamb's kidneys, roughly
  chopped
1 large onion, chopped
50 g (2 oz) lamb dripping
100 g (4 oz) button
  mushrooms, chopped
30 ml (2 level tablespoons)
  parsley, roughly chopped

salt and pepper
30 ml (2 tablespoons)
  sherry
5 ml (1 level teaspoon)
  marjoram
369-g (13-oz) packet
  frozen puff pastry,
  thawed
1 large egg, beaten

Wipe the lamb. Put the kidneys and onion with the dripping
in a heavy saucepan and cook them for 5 minutes over a
gentle heat, stirring frequently. Stir in the mushrooms and
parsley and salt and pepper to season, then add the sherry
and marjoram and cook for 2 minutes more. Stuff the leg
with half this mixture and secure it with string. Roast the
meat in a tin at 180°C (350°F)/Gas 4, for 1 hour 15 minutes,
then remove from the oven and let the meat stand for at
least 30 minutes.

Roll the pastry very thinly on a lightly-floured board to a
large square. Remove the string from the meat. Spread the
remaining kidney mixture over the pastry, put the lamb on
top, best side down, and fold the pastry round the joint to
cover it completely. Seal the edges with a little egg and make
sure all the joins will be underneath the lamb when you
serve it. Brush the pastry with beaten egg and bake it at
220°C (425°F)/Gas 7 for about 40 minutes or until the
pastry is well-risen and golden brown.

Serves 8–10

Duckling with Peach Sauce

1.5–1.75-kg (3½–4-lb)
  duckling
60 ml (4 tablespoons)
  medium sweet sherry

425-g (15-oz) can peach
  slices
salt and pepper

Wipe the duckling inside and out and prick the skin all over
with a fork. Ducks have a lot of fat on them and pricking
the skin allows this fat to run out during the roasting. Roast
the duckling at 200°C (400°F)/Gas 6 for 25 minutes to each
0.45 kg (1 lb), approximately 1 hour 40 minutes, or until the
legs are tender when tested with a fork. Remove the bird
from the roasting tin and keep hot in the oven while you
make the peach sauce.

Pour all the fat from the juices in the roasting tin. There
will be a lot of this so keep it in the fridge in a pot – it makes
a wonderfully short pastry for poultry pies. Heat the remaining juices with the sherry and the juice from the peaches and
boil for 2 or 3 minutes to reduce the amount and thicken it
slightly. Add the peaches and heat through. Season with salt
and pepper and serve with the duckling.

Serves 4

Spicy Lamb Steaks

4 shoulder steaks of lamb
  weighing 0.75 kg (1½ lb)
15 g (½ oz) butter, melted
15 ml (1 tablespoon)
  Worcestershire sauce
salt and pepper
1 clove garlic, crushed

Spicy tomato sauce:
25 g (1 oz) butter
1 small onion, chopped
1 clove garlic, crushed
425-g (15-oz) can tomatoes
5 ml (1 level teaspoon)
  basil
10 ml (1 dessertspoon)
  Worcestershire sauce

Arrange the lamb slices in a shallow dish and brush each one with butter. Pour over the Worcestershire sauce and sprinkle with salt and pepper and the crushed garlic clove. Leave for 30 minutes, turning them after 15 minutes.

Heat the butter in a saucepan, stir in the onion and cook it for 5 minutes. Stir in the garlic, tomatoes, basil and Worcestershire sauce. Break down the tomatoes with a wooden spoon and bring to the boil. Simmer for 30 minutes until the sauce has reduced and thickened. Grill the steaks under a hot grill for 5–10 minutes on each side until well browned on the outside. Taste the sauce for seasoning, add more salt and pepper if necessary and you might like to add some of the garlic marinade, too. Serve the sauce poured over the steaks.

This is a good sauce for other grilled meat and for pasta.

Serves 4

Lamb Fondue

0.75 kg (1½ lb) shoulder of
    lamb, cubed
1 small onion, finely
    chopped
1 clove garlic, crushed
salt and pepper
125 ml (¼ pint) vegetable
    oil

30 ml (2 tablespoons)
    tabasco
oil for deep frying
redcurrant jelly
mint sauce
spicy tomato sauce (see
    page 67)
aïoli (see page 47)

Put the lamb in a bowl, having trimmed off all the fat. Sprinkle with the onion, garlic and salt and freshly ground black pepper. Pour on the oil and tabasco and leave to marinate for 6 hours or, preferably, overnight. Next day, drain well and dry the cubes of meat on kitchen paper.

Heat the oil to fry the meat in a fondue saucepan and transfer it to the table. Put the sauces in small bowls, a set for each person, and divide the lamb into 4 portions. Provide plenty of skewers so that each person can dip his pieces of meat in the oil, fry them to his liking and dip in a sauce to eat.

Serves 4

Lamb with Orange Sauce

2-kg (4-lb) leg of lamb,
  boned
1 onion, skinned
1 carrot, scraped
salt and pepper

Orange stuffing:
1 small onion, chopped
25 g (1 oz) butter, melted

50 g (2 oz) fresh white
  breadcrumbs
5 ml (1 level teaspoon)
  mixed dried herbs
1 large orange
1 large egg, beaten
15 ml (1 level tablespoon)
  plain flour

Wipe the lamb. Put the whole onion and carrot in a pan with 500 ml (1 pint) cold water. Season with salt and pepper and bring to the boil. Add the shank end from the joint (ask your butcher for the bones for soup) and simmer this stock for 2 hours.

Make the stuffing by cooking the chopped onion in the butter until it is soft, then mixing in the breadcrumbs and herbs. Finely grate the rind from the orange and squeeze and strain the juice. Add the rind and half the juice to the stuffing and mix it with the egg. Use this to stuff the lamb and tie it with string.

Put the lamb in a meat tin and roast at 200°C (400°F)/ Gas 6 for 25 minutes for each 450 g (1 lb), or 1 hour 50 minutes plus 25 minutes extra. When it is cooked, remove the meat to a carving dish and keep hot.

Pour off all but 15 ml (1 tablespoon) of the fat and meat drippings from the tin. Stir in the flour and cook the gravy over a gentle heat for 2 minutes. Strain the stock and pour it into the tin, stirring all the time. Cook until the gravy thickens, then add the remaining orange juice. Season to taste with salt and pepper and serve with the stuffed lamb.

Serves 10, or 4 with plenty to eat cold next day

Sweet and Sour Chicken

50 g (2 oz) caster sugar
25 g (1 oz) cornflour
90 ml (6 tablespoons) brown malt vinegar
30 ml (2 tablespoons) pineapple juice
30 ml (2 tablespoons) sherry
30 ml (2 tablespoons) soy sauce
75 ml (5 tablespoons) oil
0.5 kg ($\frac{1}{2}$ lb) chicken, cubed
good pinch of salt
2 green peppers, prepared

To make the sweet and sour sauce, blend the caster sugar and half the cornflour with 250 ml ($\frac{1}{2}$ pint) cold water. Stir in the vinegar, pineapple juice, sherry and soy sauce. Add 15 ml (1 tablespoon) oil.

Make sure the chicken cubes are of equal size, 1.25 cm ($\frac{1}{2}$ in) long. Dry them, then rub all sides with a mixture of salt and the remaining cornflour. Heat 45 ml (3 tablespoons) oil in a frying pan and when it is very hot, add the chicken and stir-fry over a high heat for 3 to 4 minutes. Remove from the pan and keep on one side. Cut the peppers into 2.5-cm (1-in) squares. Heat the remaining oil in the frying pan and when very hot, stir-fry the peppers for just less than 1 minute. Lower the heat and pour in the sweet and sour sauce. Mix the pepper in the sauce, simmer for 5 minutes, stirring. Add the chicken and heat for just less than 1 minute. Serve at once with plain boiled rice.

Serves 4

Pineapple-baked Lamb

25 g (1 oz) butter
25 g (1 oz) caster sugar
6 lamb chops
1 medium-sized onion,
  finely chopped
213-g (7½-oz) can pineapple
  chunks, strained

2.5-cm (1-in) piece fresh
  root ginger
30 ml (2 tablespoons)
  brown malt vinegar
15 ml (1 level tablespoon)
  cornflour
salt and pepper

Melt the butter and caster sugar together in a frying pan
and brown the lamb chops on both sides. Transfer them to a
shallow ovenproof dish. Add the onion to the pan and fry it
for 5 minutes or until it is soft, then add the pineapple
chunks (reserving the juice). Peel off the golden-coloured
skin from the ginger and cut the pale green flesh into thin
slices. Add them to the pan with the onion and pineapple.
Fry for 1 minute. Stir in the pineapple juice. Blend the
vinegar and cornflour together, pour in a little hot pineapple
juice, stir and return the mixture to the frying pan. Bring to
the boil, stirring all the time until the sauce thickens. Season
it with salt and pepper and pour it over the chops. Bake at
180°C (350°F)/Gas 4 for about 45 minutes or until the chops
are tender.

Serves 6

Cream Roast Lamb

1.75-kg (3½-lb) leg of lamb
50 g (2 oz) butter
pepper
60 ml (4 tablespoons)
  boiling water
30 ml (2 tablespoons)
  white wine (optional)

10 ml (2 level teaspoons)
  cornflour
125 ml (¼ pint) double
  cream
salt

Put the leg of lamb in a roasting tin, add the butter and sprinkle the meat with pepper. Roast for 30 minutes at 180°C (350°F)/Gas 4, basting the lamb with the butter and turning it once or twice. Remove the roast from the oven, put on an ovenproof plate and keep hot. Pour off all but 30 ml (2 tablespoons) of fat from the tin.

Pour the boiling water and white wine, if used, into the roasting tin and bring it to the boil, scraping the bottom of the pan with a wooden spoon. Simmer for 5 minutes, then blend the cornflour with a little cold water and stir it into the pan. Bring back to the boil, stirring until the sauce has thickened slightly, then stir in the cream and simmer for 2 minutes. Return the lamb to the roasting tin, sprinkle it with salt and pepper and baste well with the cream sauce. Return it to the oven and cook it for 1 hour more, turning it often and basting the meat each time with the sauce. If the cream sauce is too thick at the end of the cooking time, stir in a little boiling water. Serve with the sauce.

Serves 8–10

Creamed Chicken on Rice

200 g (8 oz) cooked chicken	pepper
salt	5 ml (1 level teaspoon)
100 g (4 oz) long-grain rice	parsley, chopped
250 ml (½ pint) béchamel	5 ml (1 level teaspoon)
sauce (see page 19)	lemon rind, finely grated

Cut the chicken off the bones into small cubes. Put the bones and skin in a saucepan, cover with 500 ml (1 pint) cold water and bring to the boil. Simmer for 1 hour. Strain and bring the stock to the boil with a good pinch of salt. Pour in the rice and cook it for 15 minutes. Meanwhile make the béchamel sauce and stir in the chicken. Heat through for 5 minutes. Strain the rice and arrange it on a serving plate. Check the seasoning of the sauce, as you'll need to add more salt and pepper to season the chicken in it. Turn this mixture into the middle of the rice and sprinkle on the parsley and lemon rind to serve.

Serves 2

Gingered Apple Lamb

0.75 kg (1½ lb) lean
  shoulder lamb, cubed
1 large onion, chopped
50 g (2 oz) dripping or
  butter
15 ml (1 level tablespoon)
  plain flour

10 ml (1 level dessertspoon)
  ground ginger
250 ml (½ pint) dry cider
250 ml (½ pint) lamb stock
salt and pepper
2 large cooking apples,
  chopped

Trim the lamb of fat and bones. Fry the onion in the dripping or butter until soft. Stir in the flour, ginger, cider and stock and bring to the boil, stirring. Add the meat, season with salt and pepper and simmer for 1 hour 30 minutes or until the lamb is tender, adding the apple for the last 30 minutes. Keep the pan covered during the cooking time. Check seasoning, as you'll probably need to add a little more salt before serving.

Serves 6

Fruity Lamb with Rice

200 g (8 oz) cold roast
  lamb, cubed
1 large onion, chopped
25 g (1 oz) lamb dripping
100 g (4 oz) long-grain rice
salt and pepper

50 g (2 oz) walnuts,
  chopped
100 g (4 oz) canned
  apricots, chopped
5 ml (1 level teaspoon)
  thyme, finely chopped

Make sure the lamb is fat-free and cut into 2.5-cm (1-in) cubes. Fry the onion in the dripping in a large frying pan. Add the rice and salt and pepper and stir for 5 minutes. Add 500 ml (1 pint) cold water (some of which can be the juice from the canned apricots) and bring to the boil, stirring all the time. Reduce the heat and simmer the rice, adding the meat, nuts, apricots and thyme to the pan after 5 minutes' cooking. Continue until the rice is cooked and all the liquid has been absorbed. Check for seasoning, adding more salt and pepper, and serve piping hot.

Serves 24

Stuffed Chicken Rolls

4 breast of chicken joints
50 g (2 oz) butter, softened
1 clove garlic, crushed
6 sprigs of thyme, finely
  chopped
2 very small sprigs of
  rosemary, finely chopped
10 ml (1 level dessertspoon)
  parsley, finely chopped
salt and pepper
1 standard egg, beaten
75 g (3 oz) fresh white
  breadcrumbs
oil for deep frying

Ask your butcher to remove the wing bones from these joints. Usually they are left in so that you can tell it's chicken breast and not leg, but they're easier to handle without the bones. Beat the butter with the garlic, herbs and salt and pepper. Form the mixture into a roll and leave it in the fridge for 30 minutes to harden, then divide it into four pieces lengthwise.

Using your rolling pin, beat the chicken pieces until they are fairly thin. Put one piece of butter in the centre of the flesh side of each chicken piece and wrap the chicken carefully so that you enclose the butter completely to prevent it from running out during cooking. Tie each parcel with cotton. Coat with egg, then with breadcrumbs, patting them on well and shaking off the excess. Heat the oil to 182°C (360°F) and carefully lower in the chicken. You may have to cook the breasts two at a time. Don't use the wire basket because it will leave an imprint on the chicken. Fry them for 5 to 7 minutes until they are golden brown. Remove with a draining spoon and cut off the cotton. Drain well on kitchen paper and serve with lemon wedges and a good salad.

Serves 4

Gammon in Puff Pastry

2-kg (4-lb) gammon hock
10 ml (1 level dessertspoon)
   peppercorns
1 bay leaf
1 blade of mace
6 parsley stalks
6 sprigs of thyme

1 medium-sized onion,
   halved
369-g (13-oz) packet
   frozen puff pastry,
   thawed
1 large egg, beaten

Be sure to buy the gammon for this recipe well enough in advance, because it must marinate in its cooking liquid overnight.

Ask your butcher to bone the gammon except for the end bone. It will be easier to carve that way. Soak the gammon for 2 hours, then drain and cover with fresh cold water. Add the peppercorns, bay leaf, mace, parsley stalks, thyme and onion and bring to the boil, then turn down the heat and simmer for 20 minutes to each 450 g (1 lb). (Weigh the joint after the bone has been removed to calculate the cooking time.) Remove the pan from the heat and let the gammon cool in the liquid overnight.

Next day, remove the gammon from the liquid and take off all the skin. Roll the puff pastry thinly on a lightly-floured board to a large oblong and place the gammon on the pastry, serving side down. Wrap the pastry round, leaving the bone exposed, and seal the edges with a little beaten egg. Make sure all the joins are underneath the gammon when you turn it over and put it on a baking tray. Brush the pastry with egg and use some of the trimmings of pastry to decorate it. Bake at 230°C (450°F)/Gas 8 for 20 minutes then lower the heat to 180°C (350°F)/Gas 4 and continue cooking for another 30 minutes or until the pastry is well-risen and golden brown. If it begins to brown too much before the cooking time is over, cover the pastry with a piece of foil.

Serve hot. It's delicious cold, but you'll find the pastry wrinkles on cooling and the gammon loses some of its fantastic appearance.

Serves 16

Roast Duckling with Grapefruit

2.75-kg (6-lb) duckling
4 large grapefruit
5 ml (1 level teaspoon)
   arrowroot

5 ml (1 level teaspoon)
   caster sugar
salt and pepper

Wipe the duckling and put it on the shelf of your oven with a meat tin underneath to catch the drips. Roast at 200°C (400°F)/Gas 6 for 2 hours or until the skin is crisp and the leg meat cooked. Put on a serving dish and keep hot.

While the duckling is roasting, squeeze and strain the juice from 2 grapefruit and cut off all the peel and pith from the others. Cut these into 1.25-cm ($\frac{1}{2}$-in) slices. Blend the juice with the arrowroot and sugar. Drain off all the fat from the meat tin, leaving only the duck juices, and stir the grapefruit juice into this. Bring to the boil on top of the stove, stirring all the time until the sauce thickens. Stir in the grapefruit slices and heat them gently for 5 minutes. Season with salt and pepper and pour this sauce over the duck. Scoop up some of the slices and arrange them on top before taking the duck to the table.

Serves 4–6

Chicken Croquettes

200 g (8 oz) chicken,
  minced
50 g (2 oz) tongue, minced
1 small onion, chopped
50 g (2 oz) butter
50 g (2 oz) button
  mushrooms, chopped
25 g (1 oz) plain flour

180 ml (12 tablespoons)
  chicken stock
30 ml (2 tablespoons)
  double cream
salt and pepper
1 standard egg, beaten
50 g (2 oz) fresh white
  breadcrumbs
oil for deep frying

Mix the chicken and tongue together. Cook the onion in
the butter for 5 minutes or until soft. Add the mushrooms
and stir for another 2 minutes. Add the flour and cook for
1 minute, then remove from the heat and stir in the chicken
stock gradually. Bring to the boil and simmer for 2 minutes.
Stir in the cream and salt and pepper to season. Add the
chicken and tongue and then spread the mixture on a plate
and leave it to cool. Form it into 6 croquette shapes. Coat
each croquette first with egg and then with fine breadcrumbs,
patting them on well and shaking off excess. Heat the oil to
182°C (360°F) and cook the croquettes for about 5 minutes
or until golden brown. Remove with a draining spoon, and
put on kitchen paper. Serve with a good tomato sauce (see
page 67).

Serves 6

Duck and Orange Casserole

1.5-kg (3-lb) duckling,
  jointed
50 g (2 oz) plain flour
salt and pepper
25 g (1 oz) butter

2 large oranges
1 large onion, chopped
250 ml ($\frac{1}{2}$ pint) stock
  (made from the giblets)

Wipe the joints dry. Season the flour with salt and pepper and coat each joint thoroughly. Melt the butter in a large frying pan and fry the joints on all sides until well browned. Transfer them to a casserole. Finely grate the rind from the oranges. Squeeze and strain the juice from one and cut the flesh of the other into segments. Add the onion to the frying pan and fry until the onion is soft. Remove all but 15 ml (1 tablespoon) fat from the pan, then add any remaining seasoned flour and cook it for 1 minute. Gradually stir in the giblet stock and bring to the boil. Season with salt and pepper and add the orange rind and juice. Pour this over the duck in the casserole, cover with a lid, put in the oven at 180°C (350°F)/Gas 4 and cook it for about 1–1½ hours or until the meat is tender. Cool, then remove the solidified layer of fat, reheat and garnish with the orange segments before serving.

Serves 4

Spit-roast Lamb

1.5-kg (3-lb) shank-end leg of lamb
sprigs of mint
sprigs of thyme
1 clove garlic, thinly sliced

25 g (1 oz) dripping, melted
15 ml (1 tablespoon) honey, melted

If you haven't got a spit, cook this lamb joint on the shelf of your oven with the meat tin on the shelf below catching all the drippings.

Cut little pockets all over the fat and flesh of the lamb and insert mint in some, thyme in others (reserving a few of each for the garnish) and slivers of the garlic clove in still others. Brush with the dripping and put the lamb on the spit or on the shelf of your oven with a meat tin underneath. Roast at 220°C (425°F)/Gas 7 for 20 minutes for every 450 g (1 lb) plus 20 minutes over, or about 1½ hours altogether.

Baste occasionally with the dripping during the first hour, then finish by basting with the melted honey and leave the lamb to cook for the final time. Cut into thick slices to serve, arrange the slices on a plate and sprinkle with a couple of mint and thyme sprigs.

Serves 8

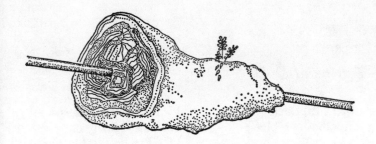

Liver Pâté

0.5 kg (1 lb) pig's liver
225 g (½ lb) unsmoked back bacon
1 medium-sized onion, chopped
100 g (4 oz) open-cap mushrooms
50 g (2 oz) butter, melted

good pinch of black pepper
good pinch of ground mace
pinch of ground nutmeg
100 g (4 oz) unsmoked streaky bacon
few bay leaves (optional)
few peppercorns (optional)

Wash the liver and cut it into chunks. Remove the rinds from the back bacon. Fry the rinds and when the fat runs, add the onion and fry it for 5 minutes or until soft. Roughly chop the mushrooms and add them to the liver and bacon. Put these ingredients twice through a mincer, though this pâté is best if not too smooth. Mix in the butter, pepper, mace and nutmeg and finally stir in the cooked onion.

Remove the rinds from the streaky bacon and use the rashers to line a 1-kg (2-lb) loaf tin. Spoon in the liver mixture, then stand the tin in a meat tin half full of water and cook in the oven at 160°C (325°F)/Gas 3 for about 1½ hours or until the pâté has shrunk from the sides of the tin. Pour excess liquid off the pâté. Allow to cool, turn out and serve as it is, or decorate the top with some bay leaves and peppercorns.

Serves 8

Terrine of Duck

2-kg (4-lb) duck
 (including giblets)
0.5 kg (1 lb) veal
90 ml (6 tablespoons)
 brandy
225 g (½ lb) fat belly of
 pork
1 large egg, beaten
salt and pepper

15 ml (1 level tablespoon)
 parsley, finely chopped
15 ml (1 level tablespoon)
 thyme, finely chopped
rind of 2 oranges, finely
 grated
100 g (¼ lb) pork fat, sliced
 thinly

Cut some of the best parts of the duck meat and a quarter of the veal into even cubes. Put them in the brandy and leave them overnight.

Next day, cut the remaining duck, veal and fat belly of pork into cubes and mince them together twice. Add the duck giblets to this mixture. Add the egg, salt and freshly ground pepper, parsley, thyme and orange rind and mix together.

Line an ovenproof dish or casserole with some of the pork fat and cover with a layer of the minced meats, then the brandied duck and veal cubes and continue to alternate layers, ending with the minced mixture. Top with more slices of pork fat and cover the dish with foil before putting on the lid. Stand the dish in a meat tin half full of water and cook in the oven at 150°C (300°F)/Gas 2 for 2 to 2½ hours.

If you want to serve the terrine at once, pour off the fat immediately it is cooked and pour in some jellied stock. This is made by boiling the duck bones with 2 pig's trotters, 1 large onion and some salt and pepper for about 1 hour until it is well reduced. Then it will set to a jelly when cold. Strain and use. If you want to keep the terrine for a special occasion in a couple of weeks' time, allow it to cool without removing the lid and foil. Then melt 225 g (½ lb) lard and pour this over the terrine to cover it completely. It will keep beautifully in the fridge until you want it. Don't be frightened of this. If you've seen those marvellous pots of Ardennes, Normandy and other pâtés in your local supermarket, they're treated in the same way and withstand long journeys and many weeks between the making and the selling of them without going off.

Serves 16

Potted Chicken

100 g (4 oz) cooked chicken	salt and pepper
	ground nutmeg
75 g (3 oz) cooked ham	100 g (4 oz) butter, melted

Mince the chicken and ham very finely. Season with salt and pepper and some nutmeg. Gradually work half the butter into the meat and press the mixture into small pots or one large dish. Smooth the tops. Pour the rest of the butter over and leave to set. Serve with toast.

Serves 4

Chicken Liver Mousse

450 g (1 lb) chicken livers
50 g (2 oz) butter
1 small onion, finely
 chopped
1 clove garlic, crushed

salt and pepper
60 ml (4 tablespoons)
 double cream, whipped
45 ml (3 tablespoons)
 sherry

Wash the livers and dry them on kitchen paper. Melt the butter in a frying pan and fry the livers until they change colour. Turn down the heat and add the onion, garlic and salt and pepper. Cook, covered, for about 5 minutes, then allow to cool. Add the cream and sherry and check the seasoning, adding more salt and pepper if required; 5 ml (1 level teaspoon) ground coriander is good too. Mix in a blender and spoon into small dishes. Chill, then serve with toast.

Serves 6

Puddings

Although you will find a lot of puddings in the Lemons and Pancakes chapters, most of the recipes are here. This is where you'll discover different ways of using rhubarb and gooseberries, lots of easy desserts such as mousses which rely on eggs, and the kinds of tarts and pies for which Britain is justly famous.

Here, for variation, I've used some store-cupboard ingredients for flavouring such as coffee, chocolate, prunes and ground almonds. Apples, oranges, bananas and grapefruit are always to be found and are so important in the preparation of puddings that to exclude them would make a very thin chapter indeed.

This is just the beginning of the fruit year – most of the best fruits are still to come but both rhubarb and gooseberries lend themselves particularly well to fools and mousses if the weather is warm and sunny, or to pies and crumbles if you still want a good hot end to a meal.

Apple and Almond Pudding

1.5 kg (3 lb) cooking
  apples
60 ml (2 level tablespoons)
  granulated sugar
75 g (3 oz) fresh white
  breadcrumbs
rosewater
100 g (4 oz) butter

100 g (4 oz) caster
  sugar
100 g (4 oz) ground
  almonds
rind of 1 lemon, finely
  grated
2 standard eggs, beaten
50 g (2 oz) flaked almonds

Peel, core and thinly slice the apples and cook them with very
little water. Allow to cool then mix in the granulated sugar
and breadcrumbs. Add a few drops of rosewater and spoon
into a shallow ovenproof dish. Cream the butter and
caster sugar until light and fluffy. Beat in the ground
almonds and lemon rind, then beat in the eggs. Spread this
mixture over the apples, sprinkle with the flaked almonds
and bake for about 1 hour at 190°C (375°F)/Gas 5 or until
the top is risen and the almonds golden. If necessary, cover
the top with foil to prevent it from getting too brown. Serve
hot, cold or, best of all, warm with cream.

Serves 8

Rhubarb Fool

450 g (1 lb) rhubarb,
  prepared
sugar to taste

Custard:
10 ml (2 level teaspoons)
  custard powder

5 ml (1 level teaspoon)
  caster sugar
125 ml ($\frac{1}{4}$ pint) milk
125 ml ($\frac{1}{4}$ pint) double
  cream, whipped
cochineal (optional)

Stew the rhubarb in very little water with sugar to taste
until tender. Blend the fruit to a purée. Blend the custard

powder with the caster sugar and a little of the milk. Bring the remaining milk to the boil, pour it on to the blended powder, stirring all the time, then pour this mixture back into the saucepan and bring to the boil, stirring all the time. Wet a piece of greaseproof paper and press it on the surface of the custard to prevent a skin from forming as the custard cools. Stir the fruit purée and the cream into the custard when cold and colour a deeper shade of pink with cochineal, if liked. Serve with shortbread or ginger biscuits.

Serves 6–8

Gooseberry Crumble

0.75 kg (1½ lb) gooseberries, prepared
40 g (1½ oz) granulated sugar
10 ml (1 level dessertspoon) lemon rind, finely grated

150 g (6 oz) plain flour, sifted
75 g (3 oz) butter
75 g (3 oz) caster sugar

Stew the gooseberries with the granulated sugar, lemon rind and 75 ml (5 tablespoons) water until just beginning to soften. Pour them into an ovenproof dish. Put the flour in a bowl, rub in the butter and stir in the sugar. Pile this mixture over the fruit and bake for 30 minutes at 190°C (375°F)/Gas 5, or until the crumble is golden brown. Serve with custard or cream.

Serves 6

Chocolate Surprise Soufflé

15 ml (1 level tablespoon)
    caster sugar
15g ($\frac{1}{2}$ oz) arrowroot
15 g ($\frac{1}{2}$ oz) plain flour
250 ml ($\frac{1}{2}$ pint) milk

40 g (1$\frac{1}{2}$ oz) plain
    chocolate
20 g ($\frac{3}{4}$ oz) butter
3 large eggs, separated
8 cherry liqueur chocolates

Blend the suger, arrowroot and flour with a tittle milk to make a smooth cream. Melt the chocolate with the remaining milk in a bowl over hot water and mix with the flour. Pour into a pan and heat, stirring continuously, until thick and smooth. Remove from the heat and stir in the butter. Allow to cool for 10 minutes, then beat in the egg yolks. Whisk the egg whites until really stiff, then fold them in using a large metal spoon. Put a 5-cm (2-in) layer of the chocolate mixture at the bottom of a buttered 18-cm (7-in) soufflé dish, then arrange the individual chocolates on this layer. Cover quickly with the remaining mixture and put the soufflé promptly into a pre-heated oven at 200°C (400°F) /Gas 6 and cook it for 25 to 30 minutes or until it is well-risen and brown. Serve with cream.

Serves 6

Coffee Milk Jelly

550 ml (1 pint) milk
10 ml (1 level dessertspoon)
    coffee powder

50 g (2 oz) caster sugar
15 g ($\frac{1}{2}$ oz) powdered
    gelatine

Pour the milk into a pan, add the coffee powder, sugar and gelatine and heat slowly to dissolve the sugar and gelatine. Strain the mixture into 1 large wetted mould or 6 small ones. Leave to set. Turn out and serve with cream if liked.

Serves 6

Praline Mousse

Praline:
50 g (2 oz) whole
  unblanched almonds
50 g (2 oz) caster sugar

Mousse:
3 large eggs, separated

75 g (3 oz) caster sugar
15 g (½ oz) powdered
  gelatine
250 ml (½ pint) double
  cream, whipped

Put the almonds and caster sugar for the praline in a small heavy pan and heat gently until all the sugar has dissolved. Cook for 3 to 4 minutes until the sugar has turned a light golden brown. Turn the almonds over and over in the caramel to coat them and pour this mixture into an oiled tin and leave to set. (It's well worth making a larger quantity of praline. The extra may be kept in an air-tight jar to be used as decoration for cakes and puddings.) When set, crush the praline to a fine powder with a rolling pin or a grinder.

Whisk the egg yolks and caster sugar until thick and fluffy using an electric mixer. If you prefer to whisk by hand, put this mixture over a saucepan of hot water and whisk until thick and fluffy. Remove from the heat and whisk until the bowl is cool. Put the gelatine and 30 ml (2 tablespoons) cold water in a basin and leave it to dissolve in a pan of hot water. Whisk the gelatine into the egg mixture, then stir in the cream. Whisk the egg whites until stiff. Fold in the praline, then fold in the egg whites. Turn this mixture into a serving dish and allow it to set.

For a special finish, sprinkle the top with plenty of icing sugar. Heat several skewers in a gas flame or by laying them on an electric element with the ends off the heat. Quickly take up the skewers holding them with a cloth and burn criss-cross marks in the sugar topping.

Serves 6

Chocolate Orange Mousse

100 g (4 oz) good plain
   chocolate
45 ml (3 tablespoons)
   warm water
4 large eggs, separated
50 g (2 oz) caster sugar

1 large orange
10 ml (1 level dessertspoon)
   powdered gelatine
125 ml ($\frac{1}{4}$ pint) double
   cream

Melt the chocolate in the warm water over a pan of hot water. Stir and allow to cool. Whisk the egg yolks and sugar until light and fluffy, by hand or with an electric mixer (see Praline Mousse). Finely grate the rind from the orange and squeeze and strain the juice. Whisk the rind into the egg mixture. Put the gelatine in 30 ml (2 tablespoons) cold water and stand it in a pan of hot water to dissolve. Whisk the gelatine into the mixture, then stir in the melted chocolate, cream and orange juice. Allow to almost set then whisk the egg whites stiffly and fold them in gently. Turn into 1 large or 6 individual serving dishes and leave to set.

Serves 6

Cherry Cheese Strudel

Quick strudel pastry:
100 g (4 oz) butter
150 g (6 oz) plain flour
40 g (1$\frac{1}{2}$ oz) caster sugar
milk to mix

Filling:
2 425-g (15-oz) cans black
cherries
100 g (4 oz) cream cheese
25 g (1 oz) almond nibs
1 standard egg, beaten
15 g ($\frac{1}{2}$ oz) butter, melted

For the pastry, rub the butter into the flour. Stir in the sugar and mix to a stiff dough with milk. Roll out very thinly, so the dough is almost transparent, on a lightly-floured board until the pastry forms a large square. Leave to rest.

Drain the cherries, reserving the juice for a sauce if you wish. Remove the cherry stones if necessary. Beat the cream cheese until it is soft, then beat in the toasted nuts and egg. Spread this mixture over the pastry, then sprinkle on the cherries. Moisten the pastry all round and roll it like a Swiss roll, using a cloth to help. Transfer it gently to a greased baking tray. Brush with the melted butter and bake at 220°C (425°F)/Gas 7 for about 25 minutes until golden brown. If liked, serve with a sauce made from the cherry syrup, thickened with 10 ml (1 level dessertspoon) arrowroot.

Serves 6–8

Grapefruit in Brandy

4 large grapefruit	60 ml (4 tablespoons)
100 g (4 oz) caster sugar	brandy
5 ml (1 level teaspoon)	whipping cream
ground mixed spice	

Using a sharp knife, cut off all the peel and pith from the grapefruit. Hold each fruit in one hand and cut between two segments through to the centre of the grapefruit. Continue in this way all round the fruit to remove the flesh, then squeeze the remaining skins to get all the juice. This method is used for preparing orange segments too.

Put the sugar in a pan with 250 ml ($\frac{1}{2}$ pint) cold water and the mixed spice. Heat gently until the sugar has dissolved, then bring to the boil and boil steadily for 5 minutes. Lower the heat, add the grapefruit segments and poach them gently for 10 minutes. Arrange the segments in a serving dish, pour over the brandy and serve with whipped cream flavoured with a little mixed spice.

Serves 6

Apple Pie

0.75 kg (1½ lb) cooking
apples
1 piece lemon rind, thinly
pared

75 g (3 oz) sugar
200 g (8 oz) shortcrust
pastry (see page 35)

Peel and core the apples, reserving both skins and cores, and slice them thickly. Put the slices in a deep bowl and cover them with water to prevent them going brown. Put the peelings, cores and lemon rind in a pan with 125 ml (¼ pint) cold water and simmer for 20 minutes. Strain and allow to cool. Layer the apples in a deep 20-cm (8-in) ovenproof pie dish, sprinkling each layer with sugar. Pour on some of the cooled apple liquid to half-fill the dish. (Water will do as well, but if you have the time, this flavoured apple liquid makes such a difference to the pie.)

Roll the pastry thinly on a lightly-floured board and cut off a strip to go round the edge of the dish. Grease the edge of the dish, press on this strip, neaten it and moisten it with water. Cover the pie with the large pastry round, pressing it lightly to the strip. Trim the edge and decorate. Bake at 200°C (400°F)/Gas 6 for 25 minutes then lower the heat to 180°C (350°F)/Gas 4 and continue cooking for another 10 to 15 minutes. If liked, sprinkle the pie with a little caster sugar as soon as you remove it from the oven, and serve.

Serves 6

Bakewell Tart

150 g (6 oz) shortcrust
pastry (see page 35)
15 ml (2 level tablespoons)
strawberry jam
25 g (1 oz) butter

50 g (2 oz) caster sugar
1 small lemon
1 large egg, beaten
50 g (2 oz) ground almonds
25 g (1 oz) cake crumbs

Roll the pastry thinly on a lightly-floured board and use to line a shallow 18-cm (7-in) ovenproof dish. Trim and decorate the edge. Spread the jam over the pastry and leave the pastry to rest. Cream the butter and sugar until fluffy. Finely grate the lemon rind and squeeze and strain the juice. Add both to the creamed mixture and beat well. Beat in the egg a little at a time, then stir in the almonds and cake crumbs. Spread this mixture evenly over the jam and bake at 190°C (375°F)/Gas 5 for about 40 minutes or until the sponge topping is springy to the touch and golden brown.

Serves 6

Orange Cream Mould

3 large oranges
250 ml (½ pint) milk
50 g (2 oz) caster sugar
3 large egg yolks

20 g (¾ oz) powdered gelatine
142-g (5-oz) carton double cream

Pare the rind off the oranges and put with the milk. Bring to the boil, then remove from the heat and allow to stand for 30 minutes. Remove the rind and stir in the sugar. Whisk the egg yolks, pour on a little milk to mix, then pour the egg yolks into the pan. Cook the custard slowly, stirring all the time until it thickens. Don't let it boil or it may curdle.

Squeeze and strain the orange juice. Put the gelatine and juice in a basin standing in a pan of hot water and leave it to dissolve. Make up the quantity to 250 ml (½ pint) with hot water. Whisk the slightly cooled gelatine into the egg custard. Whisk the cream until thick and when the custard is just beginning to set, fold in the cream.

Serves 6

Mixed Syrups Tart

200 g (8 oz) shortcrust
   pastry (see page 35)
50 g (2 oz) fresh white
   breadcrumbs
45 ml (3 level tablespoons)
   golden syrup

15 ml (1 level tablespoon)
   treacle
30 ml (2 tablespoons) maple
   syrup
juice of 1 large lemon,
   strained

Roll the pastry thinly on a lightly-floured board and use to
line a 25-cm (10-in) ovenproof dinner plate. Trim the edge
and decorate. Sprinkle the breadcrumbs over the base of the
pastry. Spoon on the syrups (or use the same quantity of
golden syrup) and sprinkle the lemon juice on top. Bake at
190°C (375°F)/Gas 5 for about 40 minutes or until the pastry
is golden. If you have any pastry left, you can always use it
by making a lattice for this tart.

Serves 6–8

Apple and Orange Trifle

5-cm (2-in) wedge of sponge
   cake
30 ml (2 level tablespoons)
   marmalade
0.5 kg (1 lb) cooking
   apples, sliced

2 large oranges
50 g (2 oz) caster sugar
250 ml (½ pint) custard
   (see page 121)
142-g (5-oz) carton double
   cream

Cut the sponge cake into small pieces and spread each piece
with a little of the marmalade. Cook the apples in 60 ml
(4 tablespoons) cold water over a gentle heat for about 10
minutes or until they are soft enough to mash to a purée.
Finely grate the rind from 1 orange and stir this into the
apples with the caster sugar. Allow to cool. Cut the oranges
into segments (see page 89) and cut each segment into 3
pieces. Arrange the oranges over the sponge in a serving dish

and pour over any juice. Spread the apple over the orange pieces. Finally pour on the custard and let it set. Whip the cream to soft peaks and spread it over the custard, marking it into a pattern with a knife. Decorate the top as you wish but pieces of crystallised ginger cut into thin slices go particularly well as do pieces of candied peel (see page 154).

Serves 8

Banana Snow

4 bananas
30 ml (2 level tablespoons) demerara sugar
10 ml (2 teaspoons) lemon juice, strained

142-g (5-oz) carton plain yoghurt
125 ml (¼ pint) double cream
3 large egg whites, whisked

Mash the bananas with the sugar and lemon juice to a smooth purée. Stir in the yoghurt and cream. Fold the egg whites into the banana mixture. Spoon into individual dishes and serve at once.

Serves 4

Prune Mousse

0.5 kg (1 lb) prunes
2 strips of lemon rind
2.5-cm (1-in) piece cinnamon stick
20 g (¾ oz) powdered gelatine

45 ml (3 tablespoons) lemon juice, strained
75 g (3 oz) caster sugar
142-g (5-oz) carton double cream

Soak the prunes overnight in 750 ml (1½ pints) cold water. Next day cook the prunes in the water with the lemon rind and cinnamon until they are soft. Stone them and blend the prune flesh with the liquid, removing the lemon rind and cinnamon stick. Put the gelatine with 60 ml (4 tablespoons) cold water in a small basin, stand it in a pan of hot water and let the gelatine dissolve. Stir the lemon juice, sugar and cream into the prune purée. Whisk the gelatine into the prune purée and pour the mixture into a wetted mould or pudding basin and leave it to set. Unmould on to a plate and serve with cream.

If you want to make this mousse for a dinner party or celebration try adding 15 ml (1 tablespoon) of sherry, port, cherry brandy or Grand Marnier instead of the lemon juice. In fact, a spot of any spirit or liqueur is good except for obvious ones, like crème de menthe, which just don't go with the prune flavour.

Serves 6

Honeycomb Mould

2 large lemons
550 ml (1 pint) milk
2 large eggs, separated

50 g (2 oz) caster sugar
15 g ($\frac{1}{2}$ oz) powdered
  gelatine

Finely grate the rind from the lemons and heat very slowly with the milk until almost boiling. Cream the egg yolks with the caster sugar and pour on a little of the milk. Add the yolk mixture to the remainder of the milk in the pan. Heat it gently, stirring all the time, then cook gently for 2 minutes, stirring. Do not let it boil because it will curdle. Squeeze out and strain the lemon juice. Put the gelatine with the lemon juice in a basin and stand the basin in a pan of hot water until the gelatine dissolves. When completely clear, cool and stir it into the custard. Whisk the egg whites stiffly, then whisk them gently into the lemon-flavoured custard as it begins to cool and set. Pour the mixture into a ring mould and leave it to set.

Serves 6

Chocolate Cherry Cases

200 g (8 oz) good plain
  chocolate, melted
142-g (5-oz) carton double
  cream, whipped
15 ml (1 tablespoon)
  brandy

10 ml (1 level dessertspoon
  caster sugar)
100 g (4 oz) cherries,
  stoned
100 g (4 oz) ripe cherries,
  with stalks

Using a small knife, spread the chocolate thickly inside paper
cake cases to build up a good case. This is easier if you leave
2 or 3 paper cases stuck together to stiffen the one being
coated. Chill in the fridge, then tear off the paper cases,
leaving chocolate replicas. Stir the cream, brandy and sugar
together. Roughly chop the stoned cherries and stir them
into the cream. Use to fill the chocolate cases and decorate
with a pair or three cherries all joined together.

Makes about 8 cases

Gooseberry Almond Tarts

Almond pastry:
200 g (8 oz) plain flour
good pinch of salt
75 g (3 oz) ground almonds
125 g (5 oz) unsalted
  butter, softened
75 g (3 oz) caster sugar
1 large egg
rind of ½ lemon, finely
  grated
almond essence

Filling:
0.5 kg (1 lb) gooseberries,
  topped and tailed
juice of ½ lemon, strained
75 g (3 oz) caster sugar

Topping:
100 g (4 oz) caster sugar
2 large egg whites, stiffly
  beaten

Sift the flour and salt into a mound on a clean work surface. Make a well in the centre and add the ground almonds,
butter (cut in pieces), sugar, egg, lemon rind and a few drops

of almond essence. Work all these ingredients together using the fingertips of one hand, drawing in the flour from the edge all the time. Knead lightly until the dough is smooth. Wrap it in foil and chill it in the fridge for 1 hour before you use it.

Stew the gooseberries lightly in 30 ml (2 tablespoons) cold water with the lemon juice and sugar, stirring them frequently to make sure that all the fruit softens and cooks but doesn't break up. Allow to cool.

Roll the pastry thinly on a lightly-floured board and use to line six 10-cm (4-in) tartlet tins. Trim the edges and fill with greaseproof paper and baking beans. Bake at 190°C (375°F)/Gas 5 for 10 minutes, then remove the beans and the paper and bake the pastry for 10 minutes more until it is golden. Allow to cool, then fill each case with the whole gooseberries.

Whisk half the sugar for the topping into the stiffly beaten egg whites, then fold in the remainder. Pile this meringue on the tarts to cover the fruit and bake at 240°C (475°F)/Gas 9 for 5 minutes or until the tips of the meringue are turning golden brown. Serve at once.

Serves 6

Orange Apple Flan

100 g (4 oz) shortcrust pastry (see page 35)	50 g (2 oz) unsalted butter
3 large oranges	75 g (3 oz) caster sugar
0.75 kg (1½ lb) cooking apples, thickly sliced	30 ml (2 level tablespoons) apricot jam, heated

Roll the pastry thinly and use to line a 18-cm (7-in) flan ring. Fill the flan with greaseproof paper and baking beans and bake blind at 190°C (375°F)/Gas 5 for 15 minutes, then remove the beans and continue baking for another 5 minutes until the pastry is golden brown. Leave to cool.

Grate the rind from the oranges. Cook the apple slices in

a saucepan with the finely grated orange rind and the butter. Cover the pan and simmer very gently, stirring from time to time, for about 20 minutes. You should not need any water, but if your heat is particularly fierce, add about 30 ml (2 tablespoons) cold water to prevent the apples catching on the bottom of the saucepan. Push the apples through a sieve, stir in the sugar, return this mixture to the pan and cook, stirring, until the apple purée is thick. Allow to cool. Cut the pith from the oranges and cut the flesh into segments (see page 89). Spread the cold apple purée in the flan case, arrange the orange segments on top in a pattern and brush with the apricot jam. Serve when cold.

Serves 6

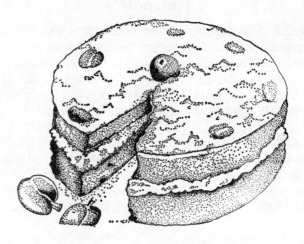

Sponges

There are several varieties of sponge cake, all of which rely on beaten eggs for their lightness. Perhaps the best known is the Victoria sandwich, made by creaming together equal quantities of fat, sugar, flour and eggs (one large egg weighs roughly 50 g (2 oz)). Then there are two sponges made by whisking – the fatless sponge and the Genoese, which is enriched with the addition of melted butter. Swiss roll mixtures are generally the whisked fatless sponge, often with the addition of a little raising agent, and the Genoese is used for a richer cake. You can of course vary these standard sponges with lots of different flavourings, and bake them in different tin shapes, too.

I've included here a few recipes for making cakes with oil; an important thing to know if anyone you cook for has been warned to watch his intake of the animal fats. Remember when you make cakes with oil that you need to use an extra raising agent, or separate the eggs and fold in the stiffly beaten whites at the last moment to counteract a slight tendency to heaviness that can sometimes occur. Also included is a truffle cake recipe for using up cake crumbs, the trimmings off Swiss rolls or the last wedge of cake that everyone politely leaves for someone else until it goes stale.

Choc-nut Cherry Cake

100 g (4 oz) self-raising
    flour, sifted
5 ml (1 level teaspoon)
    baking powder, sifted
100 g (4 oz) soft, whipped
    tub margarine
75 g (3 oz) caster sugar

2 large eggs, beaten
25 g (1 oz) plain chocolate,
    grated
25 g (1 oz) walnuts,
    chopped
25 g (1 oz) glacé cherries,
    chopped

Put all the ingredients in a large bowl and beat well to mix thoroughly, though don't overbeat (be particularly careful if you're using an electric mixer). Turn the mixture into a greased 15-cm (6-in) cake tin and bake at 160°C (325°F)/Gas 3 for about 1 hour 15 minutes or until firm to the touch and beginning to shrink from the sides of the tin. Leave to cool for a few minutes in the tin, then turn on to a wire rack. If liked, cut this cake into 3 layers and sandwich it together with chocolate cream icing (see page 101).

Apricot Gâteau

Genoese sponge:
3 large eggs
100 g (4 oz) caster sugar
75 g (3 oz) plain flour,
    sifted
45 ml (3 tablespoons) corn
    oil

Filling:
225 g (½ lb) apricots

sugar to taste
125 ml (¼ pint) double
    cream, whipped

Frosting:
1 egg white
100 g (4 oz) caster sugar
pinch of salt
pinch of cream of tartar

Put the eggs and caster sugar in a large bowl and stand it over a pan of gently simmering water. Whisk until the mixture is light and fluffy and will hold the impression of the whisk for 5 seconds. Remove from the heat and whisk until cold. Using a large metal spoon, lightly fold in the flour, then the oil and turn the mixture into two greased 18-cm (7-in) sandwich tins. Bake at 190°C (375°F)/Gas 5 for 15 to 20 minutes or until firm to the touch and beginning to shrink from the sides of the tin. Leave in the tins for a few minutes, then turn the cakes on to a wire rack to cool.

Cut each apricot in half and remove the stone. Poach the halves in a little water with sugar to taste. Allow to cool, then strain and reserve the liquid. Keep the best halves for decoration and chop the rest roughly. Beat 30-45 ml (2–3 tablespoons) apricot liquid into the cream to make it go further. Mix with the chopped fruit and use to sandwich the cakes together.

Put all the ingredients for the frosting into a bowl, add 30 ml (2 tablespoons) water and whisk. Stand the bowl over a pan of gently simmering water and continue whisking until the mixture will hold peaks. Coat the top and sides of the cake with this frosting and decorate with the reserved apricot halves.

Lemon Sandwich

Victoria sandwich:
100 g (4 oz) butter
100 g (4 oz) caster sugar
2 large eggs, beaten
1 large lemon
100 g (4 oz) self-raising
  flour, sifted

Filling and icing:
45 ml (3 level tablespoons)
  lemon curd (see page 155)
100 g (4 oz) icing sugar,
  sifted

Cream the butter and sugar together and beat in the eggs. Finely grate the rind from the lemon and beat it into the mixture. Fold in the flour and divide the mixture between

two greased 18-cm (7-in) sandwich tins. Level the mixture
gently with a knife. Bake at 190°C (375°F)/Gas 5 for 20
minutes or until both cakes are well risen, golden brown and
beginning to shrink from the sides of the tins. Turn them
on to a wire rack to cool.

Sandwich the cakes together with lemon curd. Squeeze
and strain the lemon juice and mix it with the icing sugar to
make a lemon glacé icing. Coat the top of the cake with
icing and leave to set.

Chocolate Sponge Layer

Fatless sponge:
3 large eggs
125 g (4½ oz) caster sugar
50 g (2 oz) plain flour
25 g (1 oz) cocoa

Chocolate cream icing:
75 g (3 oz) butter, softened

225 g (8 oz) icing sugar,
  sifted
50 g (2 oz) cocoa, sifted
45 ml (3 tablespoons)
  double cream
30 ml (2 tablespoons)
  warm water

Put the eggs and caster sugar in a bowl and stand the bowl
over a pan of gently simmering water. Whisk the eggs and
sugar until the mixture is light and fluffy and will hold the
impression of the whisk for 5 seconds. Remove from the
heat and whisk until cold. Sift the flour and cocoa together
and gently fold into the mixture using a metal spoon. Turn
the mixture at once into two greased and floured 18-cm
(7-in) sandwich tins and bake at 190°C (375°F)/Gas 5 for
about 20 minutes or until well risen, golden brown and
shrinking from the sides of the tins. Cool on a wire rack.

Cream the butter and gradually beat in the icing sugar,
cocoa, cream and warm water. When the mixture is smooth,
sandwich the sponges with half the icing and spread the
remainder over the top using a palette knife.

Little Sponge Cakes

100 g (4 oz) margarine
100 g (4 oz) caster sugar
2 large eggs, beaten
100 g (4 oz) self-raising
   flour, sifted

Variations:
50 g (2 oz) sultanas
50 g (2 oz) dates, chopped

50 g (2 oz) glacé cherries,
   chopped
50 g (2 oz) crystallised
   ginger, chopped
50 g (2 oz) chocolate dots
25 g (1 oz) sultanas and
   25 g (1 oz) candied peel,
   chopped

Cream the margarine and sugar until the mixture is light and fluffy. Gradually beat in the eggs, then fold in the flour and *one* of the variations, using a large tablespoon. Spoon the mixture into paper cases standing in deep patty tins or on a baking tray to the two-thirds level and bake at 190°C (375°F)/Gas 5 for about 15 to 20 minutes until well risen and golden brown.

Makes about 14

Madeleines

100 g (4 oz) butter
100 g (4 oz) caster sugar
2 large eggs, beaten
100 g (4 oz) self-raising
   flour, sifted

30 ml (2 level tablespoons)
   raspberry jam, melted
50 g (2 oz) desiccated
   coconut
5 glacé cherries, halved
angelica

Cream the butter and sugar until light and fluffy. Gradually beat in the eggs, then fold in the flour using a large spoon. Half-fill 10 greased dariole moulds with the mixture and bake at 190°C (375°F)/Gas 5 for 15 to 20 minutes. Turn out and cool on a wire rack. Push a skewer through the base of each cake in turn and brush it all over with the jam, then coat it with the coconut. Top each one with a halved cherry and a piece of angelica cut into a diamond shape to look like a leaf.

Makes 10

Chocolate Yo-yos

1 large egg
40 g (1½ oz) caster sugar
50 g (2 oz) strong plain
  flour, sifted

25 g (1 oz) butter, softened
50 g (2 oz) icing sugar,
  sifted
15 g (½ oz) chocolate,
  melted

Put the egg and caster sugar in a bowl over a pan of hot water and whisk until fluffy and thick enough to retain a trail of mixture from the whisk for 5 seconds. Remove from the heat and whisk until cool. Fold in half the flour very lightly, then fold in the rest. Quickly spoon the mixture into a piping bag fitted with a plain 1-cm (½-in) nozzle and pipe 12 small rounds, far apart, on greased baking trays. Bake at 200°C (400°F)/Gas 6 for about 10 minutes or until risen and golden. Cool on a wire rack. Beat the butter and the icing sugar into the melted chocolate and continue beating until the butter cream is very light and fluffy. Sandwich the yo-yos in pairs with this chocolate cream and dust with a little extra icing sugar, if liked.

Makes 6

Swiss Roll

3 large eggs
100 g (4 oz) caster sugar
100 g (4 oz) self-raising
  flour, sifted

15 ml (1 tablespoon) hot
  water
60 ml (4 level tablespoons)
  raspberry jam, warmed
icing sugar

Put the eggs and caster sugar in a large bowl standing over a pan of hot water. Whisk until the mixture is light and creamy and thick enough to hold a trail from the whisk for about 5 seconds. Remove from the heat and whisk until cool. Fold in half the flour, then lightly fold in the remainder with the hot water. Pour the mixture into a greased Swiss roll tin measuring 33.5×22.5 cm (13×9 in). Don't spread the mixture, but instead tilt the tin, letting the mixture run into the corners. Bake at 220°C (425°F)/Gas 7 for about 8 minutes or until golden brown and shrinking slightly from the edges. Just before the cake is done, wring out a tea towel in hot water, and cover it with a large piece of greaseproof paper. Turn the cooked sponge on to the paper, quickly trim off the edges all round using a sharp knife, spread with the jam and roll up, using the greaseproof paper to help you. If you make the first turn less of a roll and more of a fold you'll find the Swiss roll is a good shape and not too loose. Dredge with icing sugar and cool on a wire rack. Dredge again with icing sugar before serving.

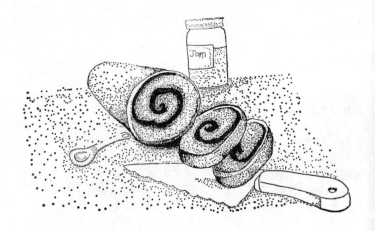

Little Chocolate Rolls

1 Swiss roll (see page 103)

Chocolate butter cream:
25 g (1 oz) butter
50 g (2 oz) icing sugar,
  sifted
15 g (½ oz) chocolate,
  melted

Chocolate frosting:
75 g (3 oz) chocolate,
  melted
75 g (3 oz) icing sugar,
  sifted

Make a Swiss roll and while it bakes cream the butter and icing sugar for the butter cream until light and fluffy, then beat in the melted chocolate. Turn the Swiss roll on to the greaseproof paper on a tea towel wrung out in hot water, but instead of rolling from one short end, quickly trim the sides, cut the sponge in half lengthwise, and roll each half from one long edge to make two long thin rolls. Leave to cool. Unroll each one, fill with chocolate butter cream, then roll up and cut each one into three pieces, using a very sharp knife.

For the frosting, melt the chocolate in a bowl over a pan of hot water, gradually beat in the icing sugar and continue beating until the mixture is very light. Put the small rolls on a cake rack standing over a clean baking tray and spread chocolate frosting thinly over each one. Allow to set.

Makes 6 rolls

Jam and Cream Sponge

One-stage cake:
100 g (4 oz) self-raising
  flour
5 ml (1 level teaspoon)
  baking powder
100 g (4 oz) soft, whipped
  tub margarine
100 g (4 oz) caster sugar

Filling:
60 ml (4 level tablespoons)
  strawberry jam
142-g (5-oz) carton double
  cream, whipped

Sift the flour and baking powder together. Add the margarine and caster sugar and beat for 2 minutes until the ingredients are well mixed. If you're using an electric mixer, be careful not to beat for too long. Spread the mixture in two greased 18-cm (7-in) sandwich tins lined at the bottom with greaseproof paper. Bake at 160°C (325°F)/Gas 3 for about 25 to 30 minutes or until both cakes are golden and springy to touch and have shrunk slightly away from the tin edges. Turn on to a wire rack by first turning the sponge on to a tea towel pad on your hand and then on to the wire rack. (Do it any other way and you will get a criss-cross pattern on the top of your cake, which isn't always desirable.) Sandwich the cooled cakes together with the jam and cream and sift icing sugar over the top to serve if liked.

Simple Sponge Cake

125 g (5 oz) self-raising
    flour
5 ml (1 level teaspoon)
    baking powder
pinch of salt
105 ml (7 tablespoons)
    pure corn oil

100 g (4 oz) caster sugar
2 large eggs, separated
60 ml (4 tablespoons)
    warm water
60 ml (4 level tablespoons)
    apricot jam

Sift the flour, baking powder and salt together. Stir in the oil, sugar, egg yolks and warm water. Stir with a wooden spoon for 2 minutes until the mixture is blended and creamy. Stiffly whisk the egg whites and fold them into the mixture, using a large metal spoon. Spoon the mixture into a greased 20-cm (8-in) cake tin with a fixed base, lined with a circle of greased greaseproof paper. Bake at 180°C (350°F)/Gas 4 for about 45 minutes until golden and well risen. Turn out and cool on a wire rack. Cut the cake into two layers, sandwich together with jam to serve and sprinkle with caster sugar, if liked.

Blender Feather Sponge

125 g (5 oz) plain flour
25 g (1 oz) cornflour
150 g (6 oz) caster sugar
10 ml (1 level dessertspoon)
  baking powder
good pinch of salt
90 ml (6 tablespoons)
  plus 10 ml (1 dessert-
  spoon) pure corn oil
2 large eggs, separated

Filling:
45 ml (3 level tablespoons)
  Ginger-up or
45 ml (3 level
  tablespoons) orange
  marmalade and
2 pieces crystallised
  ginger, chopped

Sift the flour, cornflour, 100 g (4 oz) sugar, baking powder and salt on to a piece of paper and tip them into a blender (only the large ones are suitable for this). Add the oil, egg yolks and 90 ml (6 tablespoons) water. Switch on and blend to mix. Whisk the egg whites stiffly, stir in the rest of the sugar and whisk again until stiff. Lightly fold the contents of the blender into the egg whites and divide evenly between two 20-cm (8-in) greased sandwich tins with their bases covered by circles of non-stick paper. Bake at 190°C (375°F)/Gas 5 for about 25 minutes or until golden and springy to the touch. Turn out and cool. Sandwich together with the Ginger-up or with the marmalade mixed with the chopped crystallised ginger.

Truffle Cakes

200 g (8 oz) sponge cake
  crumbs
15 g (½ oz) cocoa
25 g (1 oz) ground almonds

90 ml (6 level tablespoons)
  apricot jam, melted
5 ml (1 teaspoon) brandy
chocolate vermicelli

Mix the crumbs, cocoa and ground almonds with the jam and brandy. Form into 10 balls and coat with chocolate vermicelli.

Makes 10

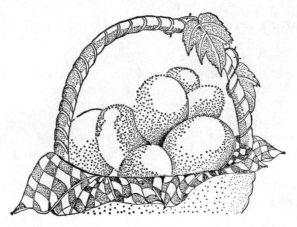

Eggs

It's at this time of the year that chickens get that certain feeling and start producing dozens of eggs, so they're usually cheaper than at other times. Make the most of this little shell packed with goodness (protein, vitamin D and minerals essential for health), one of which makes a good breakfast and costs only 4 pence at the time of writing. All the obvious ways of cooking eggs are included here – boiling, poaching, scrambling etc., plus omelettes of all varieties. So, too, are recipes for using eggs to make custard, which now has to have the adjective 'real' to distinguish it from the yellow powder kind which has become custard in most people's minds.

Eggs have the property of setting mixtures and are therefore used for flans, creams, the lemon mix of a lemon meringue pie and so on. Often either egg yolks or whites, but not both, are called for in a recipe; since making mayonnaise with left-over yolks or meringues with left-over whites isn't always what's wanted, I've suggested lots of different ways of using both.

Preserving eggs has long been considered old-fashioned

and even with freezer-ownership on the increase, there's no great move to suggest we all freeze eggs in enormous quantities. Perhaps this is because nothing yet has really superseded the bucket of eggs in water-glass. My mother always used this method and recently I've tried it for myself. It's an easy way of preserving, and the results are very good. Eggs emerge fresh from their bath even after a storage of several months, they're whole (they have to be separated for freezing) and, of course, one can always keep on adding to the bucket just as long as the eggs are well submerged in the liquid. It's the exclusion of air that keeps them; coating them with paraffin wax or pure lard will also do the trick, but this is tedious and time-consuming. Boots the Chemists are once again stocking water-glass, and if they don't have any in stock they will order it for you.

Boiled Eggs

Simmered eggs would be a better description because eggs which are boiled tend to crack. Put the required number of eggs into boiling water, lowering them in with a spoon. Reduce the heat so that it just keeps the water moving rather than boiling vigorously. Cook for 4 minutes for a light set for standard-size eggs and $4\frac{1}{2}$ to 5 minutes if you want a firmer set. Large eggs require 5 minutes for a light set and often 6 to 7 minutes for a firm set. Fresh eggs, straight from the chickens, take longer to cook than those which are bought and therefore a few days old.

Hard-boiled Eggs

Lower the eggs into boiling water, reduce to simmering point and cook the eggs for 10 to 12 minutes. When ready, they should be placed at once under running cold water until they are cold to prevent the dark discoloration between the yolk and the white and to make the shells easier to remove.

Coddled Eggs

Lower the eggs into the boiling water, cover the pan and remove it from the heat. Keep it in a warm place for about 10 minutes. The eggs will be very lightly set.

Scrambled Eggs

There are many variations of this dish. Sometimes the eggs have milk or water added to them. I prefer the recipe often called Buttered Eggs. Break 1 egg per person into a basin. Season them well with salt and pepper and whisk them thoroughly. Melt a good knob of butter in a non-stick pan and when it is hot, pour on the eggs. Using a wooden spoon, stir the eggs over a gentle heat until they begin to set. Unless you like eggs dry, this is the time to remove them from the heat, because the heat in the pan itself will continue to cook the eggs. The eggs should be creamy and moist and are good served on hot buttered toast.

For extra flavour, let the butter sizzle in the pan until it turns golden brown before adding the eggs.

Fried Eggs

Melt a little fat in a frying pan. This may be bacon fat, dripping, lard or butter. Break each egg separately into a cup before sliding it into the hot fat. Use a spoon to baste the egg with fat to cook the top at the same time as the underneath fries. Remove with a fish slice and serve. If you

are cooking bacon and eggs, fry the bacon first and keep
this hot on a plate, leaving the pan free for the eggs.

Poached Eggs

Eggs may be cooked in a special poaching pan or in a frying pan. It's certainly not necessary to buy the special poa-
cher. If you do have one, half-fill the pan itself with water.
The top for the eggs is usually shaped like a round tartlet
tin with four indentations for the eggs. Put a knob of
butter into each hollow and set it over the pan. When the
water boils, break an egg into each hollow, season them
lightly with salt and pepper and cover the pan with the lid.
Simmer gently until the eggs are set, usually about 5 minutes,
and then turn them out on to hot buttered toast.

   If, like me, you prefer the frying pan, half-fill it with water
and add a few drops of vinegar for added flavour and to
help keep the eggs in shape. Bring the water to the boil.
Break 1 egg into a cup, and pour it gently into the water.
You can give the egg a good shape by various methods.
Two effective ones are to tilt the pan as the egg goes in to
keep the white in one place, letting it set before adding
another egg and tilting the pan again, or to swirl the water
into a whirlpool with a fork and pour the egg into the centre.
The movement of the water keeps the egg in a circle while
the heat sets it before the water has stopped moving.
Lift out each egg with a fish slice, tilting the slice to drain
the egg of water before serving it.

Baked Eggs

Eggs may be cooked in individual cocottes or small ovenproof dishes. Stand as many dishes as are required on a
baking tray. Cut a small knob of butter into each dish.

Put them in the oven at 180°C (350°F)/Gas 4 for 1 to 2 minutes to melt and heat. Break an egg into each dish, sprinkle with a little salt and pepper and return the dishes to the oven until the eggs are just set, which usually takes between 5 and 8 minutes. Garnish the eggs if liked and serve at once.

Perfect Omelettes

Omelette-making is a knack which non-stick pans have simplified. Don't be put off if your first attempts aren't perfect, just make sure you stick to these rules and you'll have success every time.

Have everything ready before you begin to cook your omelette, including the person who's to eat it. It's worth getting a pan that's the right size – 15 cm (6 in) across is perfect for a 2-egg omelette. It needn't be expensive. A cheap non-stick pan is perfect, provided you keep it only for omelettes.

Break your eggs into a basin, sprinkle in some salt and pepper and beat them lightly with a fork. Put your omelette pan to heat with a 15-g ($\frac{1}{2}$-oz) knob of butter. Have ready, too, the plate on which the omelette is to be served, preferably warmed. When the butter sizzles, pour the eggs into the pan and using the back of the prongs of a fork (a wooden fork if you want to preserve the finish on your pan) draw the egg mixture from the sides to the middle, letting uncooked egg run to the sides each time. When the egg has set, let it cook for another minute or two until the underneath is golden brown. Using a palette knife, fold over one third. Slide the omelette down the pan until the flat part is overlapping the rim. Put the plate underneath the pan and tip the omelette on to the plate, folding it again as you do so. If this seems too tricky, fold the omelette in three while it is still in the pan and tip it on to the plate with the folds underneath.

Ideally the insides of the omelette should be moist; be very careful not to overcook it or you'll find it tough.

Omelette Fillings

Fines herbes: Add 5 ml (1 level teaspoon) mixed dried herbs or 10 ml (1 level dessertspoon) fresh chopped mixed herbs to the beaten egg mixture before cooking.

Cheese: Grate 40 g (1½ oz) cheese and mix 25 g (1 oz) into the beaten egg before cooking. Sprinkle the rest of the cheese over the omelette on the plate to serve.

Fish: Flake 50 g (2 oz) cooked fish such as smoked haddock and heat it gently in a little cheese sauce (see page 31). Put this mixture in the centre of the omelette before folding.

Bacon: Chop 2 rashers and fry them crisply. Drain well on kitchen paper and spoon on to the centre of the omelette before folding it.

Mushroom: Cook 50 g (2 oz) sliced mushrooms in 25 g (1 oz) butter in a saucepan until soft. Spoon them into the centre of the omelette before folding.

Tomato: Skin 2 tomatoes by dropping them into boiling water. Leave them for 1 minute, then remove and skin. Chop the tomatoes and fry the resulting pulp for 5 minutes in a knob of butter. Season well with salt and pepper. Spread this mixture down the centre of the omelette before it is folded.

Soufflé Omelettes

Use 2 large eggs for a soufflé omelette for each person. Separate the eggs. Whisk the yolks until creamy and add either 5 ml (1 level teaspoon) caster sugar and 30 ml (2 tablespoons) water for a sweet omelette or salt and pepper and the same amount of water for a savoury omelette. Whisk the egg whites until they are stiff.

Put the pan – 15 cm (6 in) in diameter – with 15 g ($\frac{1}{2}$ oz) butter on to heat. Turn the egg whites into the yolks and fold them in carefully but don't over-mix. Tilt the pan in all directions to grease the sides, then pour in the egg mixture. Cook over a moderate heat, without stirring or drawing the sides to the middle, until the omelette is golden brown underneath. Now place the pan under a hot grill to brown the top. You may put the pan in the oven but if you do, make sure the pan handle is ovenproof and the oven is pre-heated to 180°C (350°F)/Gas 4. Overcooking will toughen this omelette, so remove it as soon as it is ready. Make a mark across the omelette with a palette knife, add the sweet or savoury filling and fold the omelette in two. Turn it on to a hot plate and serve at once.

Fillings

Jam: Spread the cooked omelette with warmed raspberry or strawberry jam, fold it over and sprinkle it with icing sugar.
Fruit: Add some finely grated lemon or orange rind to the egg yolks and some heated canned fruit such as apricots, peach slices or mandarins to the cooked omelette. Fold over and sprinkle with liqueur, rum or ginger wine.
Brandy: Add 5 ml (1 teaspoon) brandy to the egg yolks, then pour 60 ml (4 tablespoons) warmed brandy around the cooked omelette on the serving dish and ignite it. Serve immediately.

Herbs: Add 5 ml (1 level teaspoon) mixed herbs to the egg yolks before cooking.
Cheese: Sprinkle 40 g (1$\frac{1}{2}$ oz) grated cheese over the cooked omelette, fold in half and serve.
Bacon: Sprinkle on 2 chopped and crisply-fried rashers of bacon before folding the omelette.

Spanish Omelette

1 medium-sized onion,
  chopped
1 green pepper, chopped
30 ml (2 tablespoons)
  cooking oil
100 g (4 oz) runner beans,
  cooked

100 g (4 oz) peas, cooked
100 g (4 oz) tomatoes,
  skinned
6 large eggs, beaten
salt and pepper

Fry the onion and pepper in the oil in a large frying pan until the onion is golden and the pepper soft. Add the beans and peas and stir to heat through. Chop the tomatoes and add to the pan. Season the eggs well with salt and pepper and pour the mixture into the pan. Cook gently for 3 minutes or until the bottom is golden and the top is just set. Cut into portions and serve flat. If you prefer, divide the mixture into 4 before cooking and make 4 individual omelettes, one at a time, in a smaller pan.

Serves 4

Farmers Omelette

1 large onion, chopped
1 large clove garlic,
  crushed
60 ml (4 tablespoons)
  cooking oil

450 g (1 lb) potatoes,
  cooked
salt and pepper
8 large eggs

Fry the onion and garlic gently in the oil in a large frying pan until the onion is golden. Slice the potatoes, add to the pan and fry with the onion until turning brown. Season the mixture well, divide into 4 parts and spoon one into a 15-cm (6-in) omelette pan. Pour in a quarter of the seasoned, beaten eggs and cook the omelette until it is golden brown underneath. Serve at once, or keep hot while you make 3 more omelettes in the same way.

Serves 4

Baked Swiss Eggs

40 g (1½ oz) butter
250 ml (½ pint) double
    cream
4 large eggs

25 g (1 oz) Gruyère cheese,
    grated
salt and pepper

Butter 4 individual fireproof dishes with 3 g (⅛ oz) butter each
and divide the cream between them. Break an egg into each
dish and sprinkle with the cheese and salt and pepper. Cover
with small dabs of the remaining butter. Bake for 12 to 15
minutes, or until the eggs are just set, at 160°C (325°F)/Gas
3. Serve at once.

Serves 4

Buttered Eggs with Haddock

50 g (2 oz) butter
8 large eggs
salt and pepper

100 g (4 oz) cooked smoked
    haddock, flaked
4 slices hot toast, buttered

Melt the butter in a saucepan. Whisk the eggs with salt and
pepper to taste and pour them into the saucepan. Stir all the
time over a medium heat until the mixture begins to thicken.
Add the flaked haddock and stir over a low heat until the
fish is hot and the eggs cooked. Pile on to the toast and serve
at once.

Serves 4

Zabaglione

3 large eggs
45 ml (3 level tablespoons)
    icing sugar, sifted

60 ml (4 tablespoons)
    Marsala

Put the eggs and sugar into the top of a double boiler or into a large bowl. Stand pan or bowl over boiling water and beat constantly for about 10 minutes or until the mixture is almost white and very fluffy. Add the Marsala and blend thoroughly, beating the mixture all the time. It should be thick and smooth. Pour it into glasses and serve it warm accompanied by boudoir biscuits or shortbread fingers.

Serves 4

Pavlova

3 large egg whites
pinch of salt
225 g (9 oz) caster sugar
5 ml (1 teaspoon) vanilla
  essence

5 ml (1 teaspoon) white
  vinegar
rhubarb fool (see page
  84)

Whisk the egg whites and salt until really stiff; fold in the sugar, vanilla essence and vinegar. Mark an 18-cm (7-in) circle on greaseproof paper using a saucepan lid as a guide. Turn the marked side of the paper face down on to a greased baking tray, then grease the paper. Using a large star nozzle, pipe the meringue to make a large basket shape, using the pencil mark as a guide and building up the sides with 2 or 3 layers. Bake at 120°C (250°F)/Gas ½ for 1 to 1½ hours until firm and lightly coloured. Allow to cool, then fill with gooseberry fool and decorate with reserved gooseberries.

Serves 8

Custard Tart

100 g (4 oz) shortcrust
  pastry (see page 35)
125 ml (¼ pint) milk
1 vanilla pod or few drops
  vanilla essence

3 large eggs
25 g (1 oz) caster sugar
nutmeg

Roll the pastry thinly and use to line a deep 18-cm (7-in) pie plate. Decorate the edge and prick the base, then leave the plate in a cool place for 30 minutes. Meanwhile, heat the milk with the vanilla pod or essence to scalding point. Whisk the eggs and sugar together until light and frothy and pour on the milk. Strain the custard into the case so that the mixture is within 0.5 cm ($\frac{1}{4}$ in) of the top, then grate some nutmeg over the custard. (Don't be tempted to fill the tart even if you have some mixture left over. It will be a disaster.) Bake at 200°C (400°F)/Gas 6 for 20 minutes, standing the pie plate on a metal baking tray. Don't overcook because this makes the custard watery.

Serves 4–6

Egg Mayonnaise

4 large eggs, hard-boiled   paprika
1 small lettuce, prepared   1 large tomato, sliced
125 ml ($\frac{1}{4}$ pint) mayonnaise
  (see page 46)

Shell the eggs and cut each in half lengthwise. Arrange a few lettuce leaves on each of 4 small plates. Put an egg, cut sides down, on each plate and coat with the mayonnaise. Sprinkle with paprika and decorate the plates with tomato slices.

Serves 4

Upside-down Cream

100 g (4 oz) caster sugar   15 g ($\frac{1}{2}$ oz) granulated
60 ml (4 tablespoons)   sugar
  warm water   2 large eggs
250 ml ($\frac{1}{2}$ pint) milk   1 large egg yolk

Put the caster sugar and warm water in a small heavy pan and allow the sugar to dissolve over a low heat and become a rich golden brown colour. Heat the milk with the granulated sugar almost to boiling point. Beat the whole eggs with the egg yolk and pour the hot milk on to them. Add the caramel, stir and strain the mixture into an oiled 15-cm (6-in) soufflé dish. Stand the dish in a meat tin half-full of water and bake it at 190°C (375°F)/Gas 5 for about 45 minutes or until set. Allow to stand a few minutes before turning out on to a serving plate. Leave to cool.

Serve with a fruit sauce, if liked, made by pushing a can of fruit and its juice through a sieve to make a purée, sweetening it if necessary with icing sugar.

Serves 4

Coconut Pyramids

125 g (5 oz) caster sugar
125 g (5 oz) desiccated
   coconut

2 large egg whites, stiffly
   whisked
cochineal

Fold the sugar and coconut into the egg whites using a large metal spoon, and tint it pale pink with a little cochineal. Pile the mixture in pyramids on a greased baking tray. Press into neat shapes or mould them with egg cups and bake at 120°C (250°F)/Gas ½ for about 45 minutes or until they begin to colour slightly. Cool on a wire rack.

Makes about 12

Floating Islands

250 ml (½ pint) milk
75 g (3 oz) caster sugar
few drops vanilla essence

3 large eggs, separated
1 large egg yolk

Pour the milk into a shallow saucepan or frying pan kept for sweets. Add 25 g (1 oz) sugar and the vanilla essence. Heat gently almost to boiling. Meanwhile stiffly whisk the egg whites and gently fold in the remaining sugar. Drop spoonfuls of the meringue on to the hot milk and poach the meringue islands for about 2 minutes or until they are just firm, turning them with a fish slice. Lift the meringues from the milk and drain them in a sieve, keeping them separate. Beat the egg yolks, then strain the milk on to them, stirring well. Return to the heat and cook slowly, stirring, until the custard thickens. Pour into a serving dish, allow it to cool, then arrange the meringue islands on top and serve.

Serves 4

Meringues

100 g (4 oz) caster sugar
2 large egg whites, stiffly
   whisked

50 g (2 oz) hazelnuts,
   toasted
142-g (5-oz) carton double
   cream, whipped

Add half the sugar to the whisked egg whites, whisk again until the mixture is stiff, and then fold in the remaining sugar. Using a piping bag with a star pipe, swirl the meringue on to a baking tray covered with non-stick paper or foil. Dry the meringues in the oven at 110°C (225°F)/Gas ¼ for at least 3 hours until they are crisp but still white. If they begin to colour, prop the oven door open a little. Crush the toasted hazelnuts, chopping them into small pieces. Fold the nuts into the cream and sandwich two meringues together with a little of it.

Makes about 8 meringues (16 stars)

Real Custard

3 large egg yolks   225 ml (½ pint) milk
25 g (1 oz) caster sugar

Whisk the egg yolks with the sugar until they are liquid.
Heat the milk to lukewarm and pour it on to the egg mixture,
stirring all the time. Strain the mixture back into the saucepan and cook it slowly over a gentle heat, stirring all the
time until the custard thickens. Do not let it boil or the eggs
may curdle. The custard should coat the back of your
wooden spoon when it is ready. If you wish, stir in a little
double cream at this stage; about 30 ml (2 tablespoons) is
the right amount. Serve with any kind of pudding or use to
make moulds and mousses.

Serves 6

Egg Whites

The classic use for egg whites, meringues, is marvellous if
your family must have a steady supply of them week in and
week out. But this is very restricting and there are dozens
of other uses for egg whites. If you have a freezer, try to
freeze them in twos or threes; if you do one day freeze an
enormous quantity, it's worth remembering that 1 egg white
equals approximately 25 ml (1 fl oz). Freeze them without
any additions and without beating. Egg whites that have
been frozen (for no longer than 9 months) make excellent
meringues.

Unwhipped egg whites may be used for glazing pastry,
and making icings for cakes and biscuits.

Whisked egg whites (besides their uses in meringues,
meringue cases, pavlovas and toppings) may be whisked into
jellies or added to batters for a light consistency for sweet or
savoury fritters. You can add them to sorbets and fruit
fools, to whipped cream to increase the bulk, to soufflés and

mousses and, as a variation of Floating Islands, they may be sweetened and poached in fruit juice and then used to top a fruit pudding.

Egg Yolks

Extra egg yolks traditionally go into mayonnaise and, as with meringues, there's a limit to the amount you can use at one time. Freeze egg yolks by stirring them (don't beat in air) and adding salt or sugar – 1 ml ($\frac{1}{4}$ level teaspoon) salt to 2 yolks or 3 ml ($\frac{1}{2}$ level teaspoon) caster sugar to 2 yolks. Please don't forget to label the carton with the number of yolks and whether they're sweet or savoury. Use within 9 months.

Egg yolks may be beaten into mashed potatoes, soups and sauces. Use an egg yolk to glaze pastry or Duchesse potatoes before baking, or beat one or two into a hot milk drink. Whisked with lemon juice, they make the Greek sauce Avgolemono which is added to a soup (see page 16,). Poach an egg yolk and slice it for garnish or push it through a sieve and sprinkle this garnish on open sandwiches, soups and salads. Many sauces rely on egg yolks – Hollandaise, Béarnaise, custard and the variations of mayonnaise. Zabaglione (see page 116) may be made using egg yolks.

Pancakes

Shrove Tuesday, or Pancake Day, is the day before Ash Wednesday, which is the first day of Lent, during which devout Christians fast. Shrove Tuesday became a kind of sorting-out day, it being the custom not only to confess (or be shriven of) one's sins but to clear the house of all foods preparatory to the Lenten abstinence. Obviously with this in mind the prudent housewife had little in the larder, being left perhaps with salt, a little flour, milk fresh from the goat or cow, and a couple of eggs laid by the chickens. It was natural to use these few ingredients to make a pancake for the last real meal until the Easter feasting.

Though today few of us fast during Lent, everyone insists that the old tradition be maintained, and on Shrove Tuesday we make pancakes. Besides this lemon and sugar recipe, you will find recipes for Russian blini, Indian paratha, Mexican tortillas and Chinese doilies, and for rolling, stacking and crisply frying the British pancake. I've also included a variety of puddings and savoury coatings which rely on batters.

Angel Puddings

50 g (2 oz) butter
50 g (2 oz) caster sugar
2 large eggs, beaten
50 g (2 oz) plain flour
250 ml ($\frac{1}{2}$ pint) milk,
   warmed

10 ml (1 level dessertspoon)
   lemon rind, grated
90 ml (6 level tablespoons)
   raspberry jam, melted

Cream the butter and sugar until soft. Beat the eggs gradually into the creamed mixture, stir in the flour, beat in the warmed milk and lemon rind and beat well. Leave the batter to stand for 30 minutes. Grease some ovenproof saucers or patty tins and pour an equal quantity into each one. Bake at 200°C (400°F)/Gas 6 for about 10 minutes or until the batter rises, then turn the oven down to 180°C (350°F)/Gas 4 and cook the puddings for another 15 to 20 minutes or until they are firm and brown on the top. Turn each pudding out, spread with melted jam and serve at once. You might like to add some cream, too.

Serves 6

Chinese Crispy Duck with Pancakes

1.5-kg (3-lb) duck, cleaned
boiling water

Pancakes:
0.5 kg (1 lb) plain flour
125 ml ($\frac{1}{4}$ pint) boiling
   water
30 ml (2 tablespoons)
   sesame or peanut oil

Filling:
12 spring onions
$\frac{1}{2}$ cucumber
250 ml ($\frac{1}{2}$ pint) soy sauce
5 ml (1 level teaspoon)
   caster sugar
30 ml (2 level tablespoons)
   blackcurrant jam

Immerse the cleaned duck for a few minutes in plenty of boiling water. Remove and dry it well, then hang it to dry in an airy place – not the fridge – overnight. (A salad shaker is useful here.) Next day, put the duck on an oven shelf and place a meat tin half-full of water below it to catch the drips. Roast at 220°C (425°F)/Gas 7 for the first 10 minutes, then reduce the heat to 190°C (375°F)/Gas 5 and continue cooking for $1\frac{1}{2}$ hours without basting. When cooked, the duck should have a crisp skin.

While the duck roasts, make the pancakes by sifting the flour into a bowl and stirring in the boiling water. Mix to a dough with a wooden spoon. Knead the dough until it is smooth, and let it stand for 10 minutes. Form the dough into a long roll and cut off 1.25-cm ($\frac{1}{2}$-in) pieces. Form these pieces into flat, very thin cakes about 7.5 cm (3 in) across, liberally flouring your board as you work. Brush the tops of two pancakes with some sesame or peanut oil and arrange them on top of each other, greased sides together. Roll this double pancake to a 15-cm (6-in) diameter round, rolling from the centre to keep the shape. Repeat with the remaining

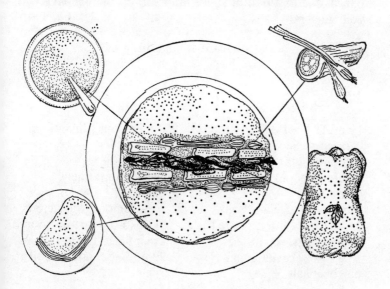

pancakes. Heat an ungreased, heavy frying pan, add one double pancake and cook it gently for about 3 minutes on each side until parts begin to brown slightly. When they're cooked, the pancakes begin to separate. Cool slightly, then pull the pancakes apart and fold each one in half, greased side inside. Continue with the rest in the same way.

To finish off, stack the pancakes in a heatproof dish, put them in a steamer and steam over a pan of vigorously boiling water for 10 minutes. Cut the spring onions into 5-cm (2-in) lengths, then split them lengthwise twice or three times depending on their size. Arrange on individual dishes, one for each person. Cut the cucumber into similar-sized pieces and add to the individual dishes. Simmer the soy sauce until it is well reduced and thick, then stir in the sugar and blackcurrant jam. Spoon about 10 ml (2 teaspoons) on to tiny dishes. Finally remove the duck from the oven, cut quickly into joints and, using a knife and fork, cut the skin and flesh into small pieces just right for the pancakes. Give each person about four pancakes.

To eat, put some duck, spring onion and cucumber on the pancake, add a dab of sauce, and roll up the pancake with your fingers.

Serves 6

Blini

10 ml (1 level dessertspoon) dried yeast

310 ml (½ pint plus 4 tablespoons) lukewarm water

325 g (12 oz) plain flour

25 g (1 oz) butter, melted

2 large eggs, separated

15 g (½ oz) caster sugar

pinch of salt

250 ml (½ pint) lukewarm milk

oil for frying

1 large onion, finely chopped

2 large lemons, quartered

2 142-g (5-oz) cartons soured cream

2 99-g (3½-oz) jars lumpfish roe

Sprinkle the yeast on the lukewarm water and leave it for 15 minutes or until it is frothy on top. Sift the flour and put half into a large bowl. Add the yeast liquid gradually and beat to a smooth batter. Cover the bowl and leave mixture to rise for about 30 minutes or until doubled in size and covered with bubbles. Gradually add the remaining flour with the melted butter. Beat the yolks, sugar and salt into the batter until smooth, then beat in the lukewarm milk. Cover and leave to rise as before.

Whisk the egg whites until stiff, fold them into the batter and cover and leave to rise again. Heat 15 ml (1 tablespoon) oil in a heavy frying pan. Add about 60 ml (4 tablespoons) batter and form it into a 10-cm (4-in) round with the tip of the spoon. Cook for about 1 minute until the underside is golden brown, then turn and brown the other side. Place on a wire rack in a warm oven while you cook the remainder of the batter.

Serve the onion, lemon wedges, soured cream and lumpfish roe in separate bowls and the blinis stacked on a plate. Each person should spoon on the toppings and eat the blini with a knife and fork.

Makes about 24

Lemon Pancakes

Pancakes: 25 g (1 oz) lard
100 g (4 oz) plain flour
good pinch of salt   *Topping:*
1 large egg   2 large lemons
250 ml ($\frac{1}{2}$ pint) milk   50 g (2 oz) caster sugar

Sift the flour and salt into a bowl. Break in the egg, add a little of the milk and beat to a thick, smooth batter. Gradually add the remaining milk. Melt a small piece of lard in a frying pan and pour in a little batter, tilting the pan immediately in all directions so that it forms a thin coating. Cook for 1 minute, then turn or toss and cook the other side until golden brown. Make 7 more in the same way.

Cut the lemon into wedges and serve each pancake with lemon and sugar.

Makes 8

Apple Pancake Layer

8 thin pancakes (see page 127)

Filling:
0.75 kg (1½ lb) cooking apples, sliced
50 g (2 oz) soft brown sugar
5 ml (1 level teaspoon) ground mixed spice
25 g (1 oz) unsalted butter
50 g (2 oz) sultanas

Honey sauce:
60 ml (4 level tablespoons) honey
juice of 1 lemon, strained
15 ml (1 level tablespoon) arrowroot
15 ml (1 level tablespoon) apricot jam

Make the pancakes as described but as thinly as possible. It's best for this recipe if they are thin enough to have holes in them. Keep them hot.

Put the apples sugar, and spice in a pan. Add 60 ml (4 tablespoons) cold water and simmer until the apples are very soft. Push through a sieve and return the mixture to the pan. Stir in the butter and cook, stirring, until the purée is thick. Layer the pancakes with the apple purée and sultanas finishing with a pancake.

Put the honey, lemon juice and 250 ml (½ pint) cold water in a pan and heat. Blend the arrowroot with a little cold water, pour on some of the hot liquid, stir and pour into the pan. Bring to the boil, stirring all the time, until the sauce thickens and clears. Stir in the apricot jam and pour some of the sauce over the pancake layer to serve. Cut into wedges and pour extra sauce round the portion.

Serves 6–8

Tortillas

200 g (7 oz) corn-meal   good pinch of salt
   or wholemeal flour

Sift the flour and salt into a bowl. Gradually pour in most
of 250 ml ($\frac{1}{2}$ pint) cold water, stirring all the time. Knead
the mixture with your hands, adding more water a little at a
time until the dough is firm and no longer sticks to your
hands. Divide the dough into 4 pieces and roll each piece
between waxed paper until it is thinner than a pancake.
Cut out large rounds, using a dinner plate as a guide.
Stack the rounds between the pieces of waxed paper,
dividing each from its neighbour. Heat a heavy frying pan or
griddle, but do not grease it. Pick each round up by its
paper, invert it into the pan, peeel of the paper and cook
each tortilla for about 1 minute on each side until both sides
are golden. Wrap 3 or 4 at a time in foil and keep them hot
in the oven. They may be cooked a couple of hours ahead
and kept hot in the oven or, if it is more convenient, wrapped
in batches in greaseproof paper, then in a damp cloth and
finally in foil to keep them moist. To reheat, brush both
sides of each tortilla with water and warm through for a
few seconds in a greaseless frying pan. If made with wholemeal flour they aren't as thin as corn-meal tortillas, but corn-
meal flour isn't available in all shops.

Makes 4

Paratha

85 ml (5$\frac{1}{2}$ tablespoons) ghee   225 g (8 oz) wholemeal
                                 flour

Make the ghee by putting 225 g ($\frac{1}{2}$ lb) unsalted butter in a
pan and melting it very slowly. When melted, increase the
heat and bring the butter to the boil. Pour into a bowl and

stand the bowl in a meat tin half-full of hot water. Place for 30 minutes in the oven at 180°C (350°F)/Gas 4. The mixture will darken slightly during cooking, but don't let it burn. You'll find the ghee is on top and transparent; the milk solids sediment at the bottom can be discarded. Put the flour with 15 ml (1 tablespoon) ghee into a bowl. Rub the flour and fat together until the mixture looks like fine breadcrumbs. Pour 45 ml (3 tablespoons) cold water into the bowl, gather into a ball and knead well. If the dough is crumbly, add more water – 15 ml (1 tablespoon) at a time – until the ball is smooth and non-sticky.

Knead the dough well, just as you would knead a yeast mixture, until it is smooth and elastic. Form into a ball put it in the bowl, cover it with a tea towel and leave to rest for 30 minutes.

Shape each paratha by breaking off a quarter of the dough and shaping it into a ball. Roll the ball into a round on a lightly-floured surface until it is slightly larger than a tea plate. Brush the top with 5 ml (1 teaspoon) ghee, fold in half and brush with about 2 ml ($\frac{1}{2}$ teaspoon) ghee, then fold it in half again to make a quarter shape. Press together and roll the paratha again. Repeat with the remaining dough, making three more. Cover with a damp tea towel and keep them in the kitchen (not the fridge) until you are ready to fry them.

Heat a heavy frying pan or griddle until it is very very hot. Add one of the parathas and cook until the top is slightly flecked with brown, keeping the paratha moving all the time. Turn it over with a fish slice and spread 5 ml (1 teaspoon) ghee over the top. Cook for 2 minutes, then turn and spread with another 5 ml (1 teaspoon) ghee and cook for a minute longer. Transfer to a hot plate, cover with foil and keep hot while you fry the remainder.

You can cook parathas earlier in the day and reheat them in a dry frying pan for a minute on each side.

Makes 4

Apple Crêpes

8 very thin pancakes   30 ml (2 tablespoons)
  (see page 127)   brandy
2 large cooking apples,   30 ml (2 level tablespoons)
  thinly sliced   caster sugar

Make the pancakes as thin as you can, so they are transparent. The apple slices should be the same. When each
pancake is cooked, fold it in half and put 1 or 2 in a shallow
flameproof dish. Cover with apple slices, arranging them in
one layer in semi-circular patterns. Sprinkle with a little
brandy and caster sugar and grill under a very hot grill for a
minute or two until the sugar caramelises and the edges of
the pancake and apple slices begin to catch. Keep warm
and finish the rest in the same way. Serve hot with cream.

Serves 8

Pancake Crisps with Spicy Yoghurt

4 pancakes (see page 127)   15 ml (1 tablespoon) clear
oil for deep frying   honey
142-g (5-oz) carton plain   5 ml (1 level teaspoon)
  yoghurt   ground cinnamon
50 g (2 oz) sultanas

This is a perfect recipe for using up a small amount of
left-over batter which isn't enough to produce pancakes with
a lemon and sugar topping for the family. Treating a few
pancakes like this makes them go further.

Cut the pancakes into strips using scissors. Heat the oil
to 182°C (360°F) or until a cube of bread will rise to the
surface and brown in 1 minute. Deep-fry the pancake strips
until they are crisp. Meanwhile, whisk the yoghurt and thin
it slightly with milk if necessary. Beat in the sultanas, honey
and spice and serve separately.

Serves 8

Fruity Batter Pudding

225 g (8 oz) plain flour
good pinch of salt
2 large eggs

500 ml (1 pint) milk
425-g (15-oz) can apricots
25 g (1 oz) almond nibs

Sift the flour and salt into a bowl. Make a well in the centre and break in the eggs. Mix with a little milk. Beat well and continue beating while adding the rest of the milk to make a thin batter. Pour the mixture into a well-greased pudding basin, cover the top with greased foil and steam it for $1\frac{1}{4}$ $1\frac{1}{2}$ hours.

Meanwhile, blend the apricots and their juice. Heat gently in a small pan when the time comes to serve. Turn out the pudding on to a plate, pour over the sauce and sprinkle with the almonds. Serve at once.

Serves 8

Crêpes Suzette

250 ml ($\frac{1}{2}$ pint) pancake
    batter (see page 127)
60 ml (4 tablespoons)
    brandy
50 g (2 oz) caster sugar

50 g (2 oz) butter
1 large orange
30 ml (2 tablespoons)
    orange curaçao
25 g (1 oz) lard

Make the batter, beat in 15 ml (1 tablespoon) brandy and leave to stand for 30 minutes. Cream the sugar and butter together until light and fluffy. Finely grate the rind from the orange into the butter, then squeeze and strain the juice. Gradually beat the orange juice into the butter until the mixture is fluffy. Finally stir in 15 ml (1 tablespoon) orange curaçao. Leave this butter in the fridge until required.

Heat a little of the lard in a frying pan and begin to fry very thin pancakes. Melt the orange butter in a large frying pan (or halve it and fry one lot of pancakes at a time), dip in each pancake and fold it into quarters. Repeat with the remaining pancakes, piling them one on top of the other in the pan until all have been dipped and folded. Continue frying for a minute or two. Sprinkle with the remaining brandy and orange curaçao, fry for 30 seconds to heat the spirits, then flame the crêpes and serve at once.

Serves 8

Gooseberry Fritters

0.5 kg (1 lb) gooseberries,   125 ml ($\frac{1}{4}$ pint)
   prepared   single cream
100 g (4 oz) plain flour   2 large eggs, separated
good pinch of salt   oil for deep frying
     caster sugar

Wash and dry the gooseberries. Sift the flour and salt into a bowl. Make a well in the centre, add the cream and egg yolks and beat well to make a stiff batter, adding 45–60 ml (3–4 tablespoons) cold water. Whisk the egg whites stiffly and stir them gently into the batter. Heat the oil to 182°C (360°F). Drop 2 or 3 gooseberries at a time into the batter, lift them out using a draining spoon and drop them gently into the hot oil. Fry the fritters to a golden brown and lift out with a draining spoon on to kitchen paper. Sprinkle with plenty of caster sugar and serve.

Serves 8

Mexican Pancakes

300 g (12 oz) plain flour
5 ml (1 level teaspoon)
  baking powder
5 ml (1 level teaspoon) salt
5 ml (1 level teaspoon)
  caster sugar
4 large eggs, beaten

50 g (2 oz) butter, melted
oil for deep frying

Topping:
100 g (4 oz) brown sugar
ground cinnamon

Sift the flour, baking powder, salt and sugar. Add the eggs
and butter and knead together to form a soft smooth dough.
Cover with a tea towel and leave in the fridge for 30 minutes.
Shape dough into 20 small balls. Sprinkle some flour on
the work surface and roll each ball to a very thin round.
Leave them to stand while you heat the oil to 182°C (360°F)
or until a 2.5-cm (1-in) cube of bread rises to the surface
and browns in 1 minute. Fry each pancake until it is golden
brown, crisp and flaky and drain it on kitchen paper.

Serve sprinkled with brown sugar and cinnamon or pour
on a little warmed honey to which you have added some
lemon juice.

Serves 8

Savoury Chicken Bake

350 g (12 oz) cold cooked
  chicken, diced
500 ml (1 pint) béchamel
  sauce (see page 19)
8 plain pancakes (see
  page 127)

340-g (12-oz) can
  sweetcorn kernels,
  drained
150 g (6 oz) strong
  Cheddar cheese, grated
ground nutmeg
salt and pepper

Stir the chicken pieces into half the béchamel sauce and heat
gently. Lay 1 pancake in a round ovenproof dish. Stir the

sweetcorn into the chicken sauce with 100 g (4 oz) of the cheese, and the nutmeg, salt and pepper to season. Spoon a portion of the chicken mixture on to the pancake, cover with another pancake and continue in this way, ending with a pancake. Pour over the remaining sauce, sprinkle with the rest of the cheese and grill until the top is golden brown and bubbly. Serve cut into wedges.

Serves 4–6

Toad-in-the-Hole

0.5 kg (1 lb) skinless   250 ml (½ pint) batter
  sausages   (see page 127)

Separate the sausages and arrange them in a greased York-shire pudding tin. Pour on the batter and cook at 220°C (425°F)/Gas 7 for 40 to 45 minutes or until the batter is well risen and golden brown.

Serves 4

Banana Fritters

4 large bananas   pinch of salt
juice of 1 lemon, strained   10 ml (1 dessertspoon) oil
                                1 large egg white, stiffly
Fritter batter: whisked
50 g (2 oz) plain flour,   oil for deep frying
  sifted   caster sugar

Peel the bananas, cut them into 5-cm (2-in) chunks and toss them in the lemon juice to prevent them browning.

Mix the flour and salt in a bowl and make a well in the centre. Pour in the oil and 30 ml (2 tablespoons) cold water. Beat until smooth, then gradually add another 30 ml (2 tablespoons) water. Immediately before you use the batter, fold in the egg white, using a large metal spoon. Heat the oil to 182°C (360°F). Drop pieces of banana into the batter, fish them out with a draining spoon and lower them into the hot oil. Cook until the batter is golden brown and crisp. Drain on kitchen paper and serve sprinkled with caster sugar.

Serves 4–6

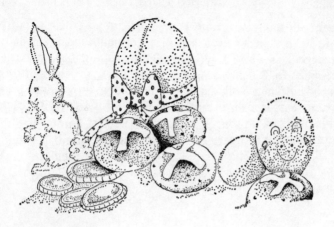

Easter

Easter, which falls between March 22 and April 25 (based on the paschal moon, which is the first to occur after the vernal equinox set on March 21), is the most holy festival of the Christian year, though many of its customs are pagan in origin. For instance, the custom of exchanging eggs goes back to pre-Christian times when eggs, as a token of renewed life, were exchanged at the time of the Spring festivals.

Hot cross buns are thought to stem from the small wheat cakes eaten at the Spring festivals in honour of Astarte, the Phoenician fertility goddess. Her Anglo-Saxon counterpart was Eostre, from which the name Easter derives. The cross on the buns, however, is of Christian origin. In orthodox households all over the world, housewives still prepare for the Easter feast; eggs are hard-boiled, dyed and decorated, cakes are baked and lamb is prepared for Easter Sunday in remembrance of Christ being the true lamb of God.

The simnel cake, which was probably first made by servant girls for Mothering Sunday in March (a traditional holiday for them), is now baked for Easter in Britain. But most other

countries have their own Easter fare. The Russian housewife bakes a yeast cake, known as Kulich, which she wraps
in a spotless white napkin to take to church for the priest's
blessing. In Portugal, the traditional sweet consists of fine
strands of egg yolk called Angel's Hair. In Poland, the
Easter feast is a huge buffet, each item blessed by the priest
with place of honour going to the Paschal Lamb, made of
butter or white sugar. The Italians bake Colomba, which is
similar to the Russians' Kulich, and the Sicilians make
Cassata alla Siciliana – layers of cake and ice cream covered
with chocolate icing.

Easter Eggs

Although nowadays the custom is to give and receive elabor-
ate and costly chocolate eggs, most countries still retain the
older, original idea of decorating hard-boiled eggs. Simplest
are those given by the Greeks, dyed a bright red, while the
Ukranians are famous for their magnificently patterned and
coloured eggs.

If you want to decorate your own eggs, choose only those
with white shells and hard-boil them in water to which you
add spinach for green, raw beetroot for red and onions for a
pale yellow. Bottled vegetable dyes may also be used, but
half to a whole bottle is required to give a good colour –
natural ingredients found in the vegetable basket produce the
best results. If you wrap onion or shallot skins round some
eggs and tie them on with cotton, the shells will have an
orange-brown mottled effect after they are boiled. Really
ambitious designs may be produced by wrapping the eggs
with masking tape before boiling in coloured water to
produce different designs on the shells. Free-form designs
may be traced on uncooked eggs with wax crayons. The wax
will melt and the designs will show up white after boiling.

Keepsake eggs should first be blown. This is something
children will enjoy. Pierce a hole at each end of an egg with

a fine darning needle, making sure the needle goes right through the egg yolk and breaks the fine covering skin. Blow through one end, puffing hard, and the egg's contents will eventually come out through the other hole. Rinse blown eggs in plenty of cold water, then warm water, blowing it through the egg. The shells can be dyed like hard-boiled eggs. These shells may then be decorated with beads, pearls, ribbons and braid and given a ribbon bow with which they can be hung as decorations. Children will love a chocolate egg within the egg shell. When the egg is quite clean inside, simply pour melted, hot chocolate through a tiny greaseproof paper funnel into a slightly enlarged hole at one end. Allow the chocolate to set and decorate the egg to cover the holes at either end.

Easter Biscuits

75 g (3 oz) butter
75 g (3 oz) caster sugar
1 egg, separated
150 g (6 oz) self-raising flour
pinch of salt

1 ml ($\frac{1}{4}$ level teaspoon) ground cinnamon
40 g ($1\frac{1}{2}$ oz) currants
15 g ($\frac{1}{2}$ oz) chopped mixed peel
milk to mix
granulated sugar

Cream the butter and sugar together, then beat in the egg yolk. Sift the flour, salt and cinnamon and fold this mixture alternately with the currants and peel into the creamed butter. Mix with some milk to a fairly soft dough, then cover and leave in the fridge to become firm. Knead lightly on a floured board and roll out to 0.5-cm ($\frac{1}{4}$-in) thickness. Cut into rounds using a 6-cm ($2\frac{1}{2}$-in) fluted cutter. Arrange on greased baking trays, bake at 200°C (400°F)/Gas 6 for 10 minutes, then brush with lightly beaten egg white and sprinkle with granulated sugar. Return biscuits to the oven for another 5 to 10 minutes or until lightly coloured.

Makes about 20

Hot Cross Buns

7 g ($\frac{1}{4}$ oz) dried yeast
125 ml ($\frac{1}{4}$ pint) warm water
350 g (12 oz) plain strong
   white flour
5 ml (1 level teaspoon) salt
40 g ($1\frac{1}{2}$ oz) lard
10 ml (1 level dessertspoon)
   ground mixed spice

3 ml ($\frac{1}{2}$ level teaspoon)
   ground cinnamon
75 g (3 oz) caster sugar
75 g (3 oz) sultanas
25 g (1 oz) chopped mixed
   peel
1 large egg, beaten
30 ml (2 tablespoons) milk

Sprinkle the dried yeast on to the warm water and leave for 15 minutes or until frothy. Sift the flour and salt and rub in the lard. Stir in the spices and 50 g (2 oz) sugar, the sultanas and peel. Add the egg to the yeast mixture and use to mix the flour to a fairly soft dough. Knead the dough on a lightly floured surface and put it into an oiled polythene bag. Leave to rise in a warm place for about 1 hour or until it has doubled in size. If the dough is stringy when you pull at a piece, it's ready. Knead it well again on a floured surface and divide the mixture into 12 equal pieces. Shape each piece into a bun and place them 5 cm (2 in) apart on greased baking trays. Using a sharp knife, cut a cross on top of each bun. Put the buns in a warm place for about 15 minutes to prove, then re-mark the crosses if necessary and bake at 220°C (425°F)/Gas 7 for about 15 minutes or until golden brown. Brush with a glaze made by dissolving the remaining sugar in the milk.

Makes 12

Simnel Cake

225 g (8 oz) plain flour
pinch of salt
5 ml (1 level teaspoon)
  baking powder
5 ml (1 level teaspoon)
  ground cinnamon
5 ml (1 level teaspoon)
  ground nutmeg
225 g (8 oz) sultanas
225 g (8 oz) currants
100 g (4 oz) chopped
  mixed peel
50 g (2 oz) glacé cherries,
  chopped
175 g (6 oz) butter

175 g (6 oz) caster sugar
3 large eggs, beaten
milk to mix

Almond paste:
175 g (6 oz) ground
  almonds
75 g (3 oz) caster sugar
75 g (3 oz) icing sugar,
  sifted
2 large egg yolks
60 ml (4 level tablespoons)
  apricot jam, melted
Easter decorations and
  ribbon

Sift the flour, salt, baking powder and spices. Mix the dried fruit with the peel and cherries. Cream the butter and sugar together, then beat in the eggs. Alternately fold the flour and fruit mixtures into the creamed butter, then mix to a stiff dropping consistency with some milk. Turn the mixture into a 20-cm (8-in) round cake tin greased and lined with greased greaseproof paper. Make a depression in the centre of the mixture so the baked cake will have a flat top. Bake at 160°C (325°F)/Gas 3 for 2 hours or until a warm skewer comes out clean after testing. Leave to cool in the tin, then turn the cake on to a wire cake rack.

Mix the ground almonds and the two sugars to a paste with the egg yolks. Reserve a quarter of the paste and roll the remainder to fit the top of the cake. Brush the cake top with some of the apricot jam, put the almond paste in place and neaten the sides where it joins the cake. Form the remaining almond paste into 11 balls (one for each faithful disciple). Brush the top of the cake with the remaining jam and arrange the balls around the edge. Brush with jam and, if the simnel cake is not too high, put it under your grill to lightly brown the topping.

Arrange Easter decorations such as chicks, rabbits or eggs in the centre and tie the ribbon round the cake to finish.

Somerset Easter Cakes

100 g (4 oz) butter
200 g (8 oz) plain flour
100 g (4 oz) currants
100 g (4 oz) caster sugar
3 ml ($\frac{1}{2}$ level teaspoon) ground cinnamon

3 ml ($\frac{1}{2}$ level teaspoon) ground mixed spice
1 standard egg, beaten
30 ml (2 tablespoons) brandy

Rub the butter into the flour then stir in the currants, sugar, cinnamon and mixed spice. Mix to a stiff dough with the egg and brandy and knead lightly until smooth. Roll out on a lightly-floured board to a 1·5-cm ($\frac{1}{2}$-in) thickness and cut into 7-cm (3-in) rounds. Arrange on greased baking trays and bake at 180°C (350°F)/Gas 4 for about 20 minutes. Don't let them cook long enough to colour; if you do, they'll be crisp and not as good as when they're soft and scone-like.

Makes 10

Greek Easter Bread

20 g ($\frac{3}{4}$ oz) dried yeast
45 ml (3 tablespoons) lukewarm milk
325 g (12 oz) plain flour
50 g (2 oz) caster sugar
good pinch of salt

2 large eggs, beaten
100 g (4 oz) butter, cut in pieces
5 ml (1 level teaspoon) lemon rind, finely grated

Sprinkle the yeast on the milk and leave it to stand in a warm place for about 10 minutes or until it doubles in size. Sift 225 g (8 oz) plain flour into a bowl, stir in the sugar and salt and make a well in the centre. Add the yeast liquid and the eggs and gradually draw in the flour using a wooden spoon. Beat well until the mixture is smooth. Beat in the butter and lemon rind and at the same time add the remaining flour – 30 ml (2 tablespoons) at a time – to form a soft dough. Use your hands to work in the last of the flour. Knead the dough on a lightly-floured surface for about 10 minutes until it is smooth and elastic. Flour the board (little and often is the clue to keep it from sticking) while you knead. Shape the dough into a ball and put it inside a large oiled polythene bag, puffing up the bag to keep it from touching the dough. Leave it in a warm place for about 2 hours or until the dough doubles in size.

Grease a baking tray well. Knead the dough again on the working surface and form it into a long roll about 5 cm (2 in) in diameter. Arrange one end of the sausage into a ring about 15 cm (6 in) in diameter, then continue in smaller and smaller circles building the dough into a rolled cone shape.

Form this cone on the baking tray, because you'll find it tricky to move it from the work surface. Let the loaf rise in a warm place, uncovered, for about 30 minutes; brush it with a little left-over beaten egg or milk, then bake it at 180°C (350°F)/Gas 4 for about 50 minutes or until it is golden brown. Cool on a rack.

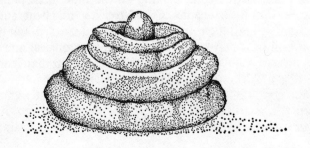

I have seen this bread served at Easter in Greece with a hard-boiled egg, dyed red, pushed into the centre of the coils. If you want to do this, add the egg after the final rising process, before you bake the dough.

Russian Cheese Sweet

0.75 kg (1½ lb) cottage
  cheese
25 g (1 oz) candied fruit,
  chopped
few drops vanilla essence
100 g (4 oz) unsalted butter,
  softened

142-g (5-oz) carton double
  cream
2 egg yolks
75 g (3 oz) caster sugar
25 g (1 oz) almonds,
  finely chopped

Drain the cottage cheese of all liquid by putting it in a fine sieve, covering it with a piece of muslin or clean handkerchief and weighting it with a 1-kg (2-lb) can of fruit. Leave it for 4 hours to drain. Put the candied fruit and a few drops of vanilla essence in a bowl, stir and leave it until the cheese is ready. (If you have any crystallised fruits left from Christmas, use these. If not, use good quality candied peel.)

Rub the cheese through the sieve, using a wooden spoon, and beat in the butter. Heat the cream until bubbles form, then remove from the heat. Whisk the egg yolks and sugar for about 8 minutes or until the mixture thickens and begins to hold a shape when the whisk is lifted out. Slowly add the cream in a thin stream, beating all the time, then pour the mixture into the saucepan. Cook over a gentle heat, stirring constantly, until the mixture thickens to a custard, but don't let it boil or it may curdle. Stir in the fruit or peel and cool the custard quickly, stirring it all the time so that it won't develop a skin on the surface. When it is completely cool, fold it gently into the cottage cheese and add the almonds. Turn the mixture into a muslin-lined sieve and cover the surface with the muslin. Stand the sieve over a basin and place a small cake tin inside the rim, then weight it with as many cans of fruit as you can balance in the cake tin. Put the whole contraption in the fridge and leave it overnight until the sweet is firm.

Next day, turn out the mould, peel off the muslin and decorate it, if you like, with toasted almond flakes.

Serves 8

Italian Easter Cake

75 g (3 oz) sultanas
75 g (3 oz) seedless raisins
60 ml (4 tablespoons) rum
100 g (4 oz) sponge cake
  crumbs
75 g (3 oz) chopped
  mixed nuts
75 g (3 oz) chopped
  candied peel
50 g (2 oz) caster sugar
10 ml (2 teaspoons) lemon
  juice, strained
213-g (7½-oz) packet frozen
  puff pastry, thawed
1 large egg
25 g (1 oz) butter, melted
ground cinnamon

Put the sultanas and raisins in a basin, pour on the rum and leave them to soak until they have absorbed all the spirit. Mix in the cake crumbs, nuts, peel, sugar and lemon juice. Roll the puff pastry on a lightly-floured board to an oblong about twice the size and half the thickness of the original block. Put the pastry on a baking tray and spread it with the fruit mixture. Beat the egg and butter together until well mixed. Pour this over the top and sprinkle with ground cinnamon. Bake at 230°C (450°F)/Gas 8 for about 20 minutes then at 200°C (400°F)/Gas 6 for 30 minutes or until the pastry is cooked and the top golden. Serve hot or cold.

Serves 6

Russian Kulich

25 g (1 oz) dried yeast
90 ml (6 tablespoons)
   lukewarm milk
25 g (1 oz) sultanas
40 ml (4 dessertspoons) rum
12 stamens of saffron
100 g (4 oz) icing sugar
325 g (12 oz) plain flour
good pinch of salt
few drops vanilla essence

5 egg yolks, beaten
100 g (4 oz) unsalted butter,
   softened
25 g (1 oz) almond nibs,
   toasted
25 g (1 oz) crystallised
   fruit or candied peel
lemon glacé icing (see
   page 100)

Sprinkle the yeast on the milk and leave it for about 10 minutes or until it has doubled in size. Soak the sultanas in the rum and add the saffron stamens. Sift the icing sugar, 225 g (8 oz) flour and salt into a mixing bowl. Make a well in the centre and pour in the yeasty milk, a few drops of vanilla essence, the egg yolks, and the rum drained from the sultanas and saffron. Beat the mixture with a wooden spoon until it forms a soft dough. Cut the butter into pieces and beat them into the dough.

Knead the dough on a lightly-floured surface, adding the remaining flour a spoonful at a time. Continue to knead until the dough is smooth and no longer sticky. Put the dough into an oiled polythene bag, puffing it out so that it doesn't touch the dough and leave it in a warm place for at least 2 hours or until it doubles in size.

Pick the saffron stamens out of the sultanas and combine the sultanas with the nuts and fruit or peel. When the dough is ready, knock it back and knead it thoroughly, kneading in the mixed fruit. Turn the dough into a greased 18-cm (7-in) cake tin with a loose base and leave it in a warm place for about 30 minutes to rise again. Bake at 200°C (400°F)/Gas 6 for about 15 minutes, then reduce the heat to 180°C (350°F)/Gas 4 and bake for another hour. Cool on a wire rack, but only while you make the icing. When ready, ice

the Kulich with lemon-flavoured glacé icing, letting it
dribble down the sides.

Serves 8

Russian Hazelnut Cake

5 eggs, separated   *Topping:*
125 g (5 oz) caster sugar   142-g (5-oz) carton double
1 large lemon   cream
225 g (8 oz) hazelnuts,   30 ml (2 tablespoons) rum
   toasted   30 ml (2 level tablespoons)
                                     icing sugar, sifted

Whisk the egg yolks and caster sugar for at least 10 minutes
or until the mixture is thick and creamy and when you lift
the whisk it leaves a trail. Finely grate the lemon rind and
squeeze and strain the juice. Grind the nuts in a coffee
grinder and fold them with the lemon rind and juice into
the egg mixture. Whisk the egg whites until they are stiff but
not completely dry and fold them into the mixture. Pour
this mixture into a very well buttered 15-cm (6-in) cake tin
with a fixed base and spread it lightly, but only if really
necessary, with a spatula. Bake at 190°C (375°F)/Gas 5 for
45 minutes or until it has puffed up and come slightly
away from the sides of the tin. Turn off the oven and leave
the cake there for 15 minutes. Remove and cool for 10 minutes, then carefully turn it on to a cake rack – first turn it on
to a tea cloth on your hand, then put the cake rack against
the base of the cake and turn the whole thing over.
   Whisk the cream and beat in the rum and icing sugar, beating until the mixture is stiff. Spread this over the top of the
cold cake and serve it at once.

Serves 8

Greek Easter Lamb

1.5 kg (3 lb) best end neck
  of lamb, in one piece
50 g (2 oz) butter
salt and pepper
½ large lemon

0.5 kg (1 lb) small onions,
  skinned
1 clove garlic, finely
  chopped

Wipe the meat and cut it into six serving pieces. Melt the butter in a roasting tin. Rub the meat pieces with salt and pepper and the cut side of the lemon. Put them in the roasting tin and roast at 180°C (350°F)/Gas 4 for 30 minutes, basting occasionally with the butter. While the lamb cooks, skin the onions, leaving them whole if really small, or cutting them in halves if they are medium-sized. Put the onions in the roasting tin around the meat and sprinkle the garlic pieces over the meat. Season again with salt and pepper, squeeze any juice remaining in the lemon half over the meat and return to the oven to roast for another 30 to 45 minutes. The Greeks like their lamb cooked until it is falling off the bone.

Serves 6

Preserves

There's not a lot of preserving to do at this time of the year, so it's worth spending some time with lemons, rhubarb and gooseberries and filling the shelves with a few pots of pickles and jams before the real season starts in the summer. While lemons are plentiful and not too expensive, make lemon curd – and for something that's a little bit different, pickle lemons to serve with fish dishes and curries. Two other easy pickles are eggs and prunes, the first an old-fashioned pub favourite and the second, less well known, a delicious accompaniment to cold meats, meat pies and salad dishes.

Rhubarb lends itself so well not only to jam, ideally with the addition of ginger to perk up the flavour, but to jellies, flavoured with mint to be served with the new lamb, and to make a ketchup. This is another old-fashioned recipe, once belonging firmly in the housewife's repertoire but now largely forgotten in these days of bought preserves. Gooseberries in this chapter are made into jam and a relish for cold-meat days and preserved orange slices will decorate many puddings, form a delicious caramelised topping for upside-down sponge puddings and make a special sweet on their own.

Finally, a quick candied peel which I add to cakes and puddings instead of the bought variety. It's cheap because it uses the discarded peels from oranges, lemons, tangerines and grapefruit. I mix them up sometimes, but if I'm being really thrifty and using every scrap of peel after each fruit has been eaten, I make separate pots which add their own individual flavours to my baking.

Minty Rhubarb Jelly

1.35–1.60-kg (3–3½-lb)
  young rhubarb, chopped
preserving or granulated
  sugar

12 long stalks of young
  mint
juice of 2 lemons, strained

Put the rhubarb in a large pan and add 1 litre (1¾ pints) cold water. Bring slowly to the boil, then simmer gently for about 1 hour or until the fruit is soft and pulpy. Strain the pulp through three layers of muslin into a large bowl. Don't squeeze the bag or try to hurry the juice along by pushing it through because your jelly will be cloudy. It's ideal to let it drain overnight. Put the pulp back into the saucepan, add 500 ml (1 pint) cold water and stew the fruit again, breaking it down with a wooden spoon. Strain the pulp as before, mixing the two batches of fruit juices. Measure it (approx. 1.75 litres (3 pints)) into a clean pan and add 450 g (1 lb) sugar to each 500 ml (1 pint) of juice. Stir the mixture over a gentle heat until the sugar has completely dissolved. Wash the mint and add it to the pan (tied in a bundle to make it easy to remove later) with the lemon juice. Boil the jelly for about 20 minutes or until setting point is reached. Test for a set by putting a little on a saucer (remove the pan from the heat while you do this because the jelly could boil past setting point which is wasteful). When cold, see if it wrinkles when you push your finger through it. Pour into warm, clean jam jars, cover the jelly surface with a waxed disc, then the jars with transparent covers. Label and store. Serve with lamb as a change from mint sauce and redcurrant jelly.

Makes 1.8 kg (4 lb) jelly

Gooseberry Relish

2.75 kg (6 lb) gooseberries
0.5 kg (1 lb) onions, chopped
0.5 kg (1 lb) seedless raisins
25 g (1 oz) salt

15 ml (1 level tablespoon) ground mixed spice
900 g (2 lb) sugar
750 ml (1½ pints) malt vinegar

Top and tail the gooseberries (ripe ones are ideal for this recipe) and put them in a large pan with all the other ingredients. Bring to the boil slowly, stirring all the time, until the sugar has dissolved, then simmer until the chutney is thick and there is no free vinegar. This will take at least an hour, so stir the mixture occasionally. Bottle, seal and label, and store in a cool place.

Makes about 3·1 kg (7 lb)

Rhubarb Ketchup

1 kg (2½ lb) rhubarb, prepared
200 g (½ lb) onions, chopped
250 ml (½ pint) white vinegar
10 ml (2 level teaspoons) salt

5 ml (1 level teaspoon) paprika
5 cloves
10 ml (2 level teaspoons) ground cumin
450 g (1 lb) sugar

Put the rhubarb and onions in a large heavy pan. Add

125 ml ($\frac{1}{4}$ pint) vinegar and cook the mixture slowly until the onions are very soft. Stir in the salt, paprika, cloves and cumin and continue to cook until the mixture will sieve easily. You can use a blender (tie the cloves in a piece of muslin and retrieve before blending) but the sauce won't be as smooth as a sieved one. Return the sieved mixture to the rinsed pan, stir in the sugar and remaining vinegar and boil for about 45 minutes or until the sauce is smooth and thick. Bottle and sterilise.

Choose small jars with screw-tops. Wash them first, then boil the jars and caps for 15 minutes. Use the handle of your wooden spoon to remove the jars from the water and drain upside down, then put right side up on a wooden surface. Fill with ketchup to within 2.5 cm (1 in) of the top and lightly seal with the screw-tops at once. Sterilise the bottles by standing them in water up to their necks on wadded newspaper in a deep saucepan. Make sure the bottles don't touch each other or the sides of the pan. Bring the water to the boil and maintain the temperature at 77°C (170°F) for 30 minutes. If you don't have a thermometer, bring the water to a fast boil and keep it bubbling vigorously for 20 minutes at least. Top up the water if necessary with more boiling water. Remove the bottles using oven gloves and tighten the screw-tops completely and leave to cool. For a complete seal, dip each bottle top in melted candle wax and store the ketchup in a cool, dark place. Once opened, it will keep for about 2 weeks, hence the advice to save all your small jars and use those for this recipe.

Makes about 550 ml (1 pint)

Ginger Rhubarb Jam

1.35 kg (3 lb) rhubarb, prepared
1.35 kg (3 lb) preserving sugar
25 g (1 oz) root ginger, bruised

100 g (4 oz) crystallised or preserved ginger, diced

Layer the rhubarb with the sugar in a large bowl; cover and leave overnight. Tie the root ginger in a piece of muslin and put it in a preserving or large pan with the rhubarb, sugar and juice from the bowl. Bring to the boil and boil fast for 15 minutes. Remove the root ginger, add the crystallised or preserved ginger pieces and boil for 5 minutes or until setting point is reached. Test for a set by removing the pan from the heat, putting a small amount of jam on a plate and cooling it quickly in the fridge. When cool it will wrinkle when you push the jam with your finger if setting point has been reached. Pour into heated jam jars, cover with waxed discs and cellophane circles, label and store the jam in a cool, dark place.

Makes about 2·25 kg (5 lb)

Gooseberry Jam

2.5 kg (6 lb) slightly
   under-ripe gooseberries

2.5 kg (6 lb) preserving
   sugar

Top and tail the gooseberries and put them in a preserving or large pan with 1 litre (1¾ pints) water. Simmer for about 30 minutes or until the fruit is really soft. Mash it to a pulp with a wooden spoon and stir it occasionally as it cooks. Add the sugar and let it dissolve over a low heat, stirring all the time, then boil rapidly until setting point is reached. Test for a set as described in Minty Rhubarb Jelly.

Makes about 4·5 kg (10 lb)

Pickled Lemons

6 large lemons
100 g (4 oz) salt
750 ml (1½ pints) white
   malt vinegar

12 peppercorns
2 pieces of dried root ginger
2 cloves garlic, skinned

Wipe the lemons and cut them into even-sized chunks, removing the pips. Rub the salt into all the cut edges and leave the lemons in a large bowl, covered with a tea towel and sitting in the fridge, for 5 days or until all the salt has dissolved with the lemon juice to form a liquid. Drain off this liquid and add enough vinegar to it to cover the lemon pieces. Bring the salty vinegar to the boil with the peppercorns and root ginger, skimming it while it boils for 10 minutes. Put the lemon pieces in a wide-neck jar with a screw-top (one previously used for holding pickles is ideal) and when the vinegar is cool pour it in the jar to cover the fruit. Push the garlic cloves down into the bottle and screw on the top. Serve with curries and with fish dishes.

Quick Candied Peel

When lemons and oranges are plentiful and reasonably cheap, it seems more of a waste than ever to throw away the peel, particularly when it's so bright and free of blemishes. Don't waste any. Finely grated lemon, orange and grapefruit peel can be packed into small boxes (the kind which contain an individual serving of butter or jam) and frozen until you require it.

If you haven't got a freezer, here's a way of making delicious-tasting peel for cakes and saving yourself some cash at the same time. Using a very sharp knife, cut the rind from oranges, lemons, grapefruit and tangerines when they are in season. Then turn the peel over and cut off any white pith. Cut the rind into small pieces. Put the pieces in a screw-top jar, add enough golden syrup to keep the rind covered and, ideally, store in the fridge. Use within 6 months. This peel is no sweeter than bought candied peel so there is no need to adjust your favourite cake recipes. 15 ml (1 level tablespoon) equals approximately 25 g (1 oz).

Pickled Prunes

1 kg (2 lb) large prunes
500 ml (1 pint) brown
  malt vinegar
225 g (½ lb) granulated
  sugar

6 peppercorns
1 blade of mace
1 piece of dried root ginger

Soak the prunes in plenty of cold water at least overnight until they are plump and smooth-looking. When they are ready, drain off the water and pack them into large screwtop jars. Use jars which once contained pickles because the lid will have a coating which prevents the vinegar leaking and evaporating. Ordinary jam jar lids don't have this. Put the vinegar, sugar, peppercorns, mace and ginger in a pan and bring it to the boil, then simmer gently for 15 minutes. Pour the hot spicy vinegar (complete with the spices) over the prunes and screw on the lids. Make sure the prunes are completely covered with the vinegar. Keep these prunes for as long as you can – three months is good, six is even better. Serve them with cold meats, pâtés and pork roasts.

Lemon Curd

4 large lemons
450 g (1 lb) caster sugar

100 g (4 oz) butter
4 large eggs, beaten

Carefully grate the rind from the lemons so that only the yellow zest is removed and none of the white pith. Squeeze and strain the juice into the top of a double saucepan or into a basin standing over a pan of hot water. Add the rind, sugar, butter and eggs and simmer gently, stirring all the time until the sugar has dissolved. Continue to simmer gently, stirring all the time, until the curd will coat the back of the wooden spoon. Pot and cover and store in a cool place.

Makes about 675 g (1½ lb)

Preserved Orange Slices

8 medium-sized oranges   250 ml ($\frac{1}{2}$ pint) dry white
1 kg (2 lb) granulated sugar   wine

Thin-skinned oranges are best for this recipe. Wipe the skins and cut the oranges into 0.5-cm ($\frac{1}{4}$-in) slices, discarding the ends. Use only those slices which have a lot of flesh in them. Dig out the pips using a skewer. Arrange the slices in two layers in a dish, cover them with the sugar and leave overnight. Next day put the oranges and sugar syrup in a heavy saucepan and bring them to the boil. You may need to add a little water – if you do, add 15 ml (1 tablespoon) at a time. Too much water will spoil this recipe. Cook the oranges until the peel is tender and they look slightly transparent. Pour in the wine and stir gently so that you don't break the slices. Put the slices into wide-necked screw-top jars and screw down the caps. You'll find the oranges set lightly. Use them as a pudding on their own with whipped cream, as a sauce for batter puddings and mousses or as decoration. The orange wine syrup should be thickened if the slices are served on their own as a pudding. 5 ml (1 level teaspoon) arrowroot to 225 ml ($\frac{1}{2}$ pint) syrup will be sufficient.

Serves 8

Pickled Eggs

24 eggs   1 litre (2 pints) brown malt
                             vinegar

If you ever get new-laid eggs, keep them for a few days before attempting to hard-boil them. When new, they're very difficult to shell.

    Hard-boil the eggs for 10 minutes and boil the vinegar

separately. When the eggs are cooked put them under running cold water to cool; this prevents the dark ring forming round the yolk, which spoils the appearance. Remove the shells and pack the eggs into a large wide-necked jar, one that has been used for pickles because the screw-cap will withstand the effects of the vinegar. Pour on the hot vinegar and screw on the top. Keep for 4 weeks before eating. The outside of the eggs should be a creamy brown colour and the insides fairly soft. If you don't have enough vinegar to cover the eggs, simply boil some more. And you can always add more eggs when they're cheap. Serve with cold meats, bread and cheese and ale.

Lemons

Although lemons are imported all year round, the largest amounts come to us at this time of the year from Israel, so you'll find Jaffa lemons in the shops until May. They should be cheaper during the Spring months, but, when everything is pence dearer than it was last Spring, I find it impossible to tell if the price of seasonal produce will come down further or if it's already in mid-glut and at rock-bottom prices. However, lemons are more expensive during the other months of the year, so buy them now and use them a lot.

Lemons contribute a distinctive flavour and the recipes in this chapter show what a variety of dishes – both sweet and savoury – benefit from the addition of lemon juice, grated rind or both. Try, too, some lemon barley water – an old-fashioned drink prescribed to purify the blood. Mother always insisted I needed this remedy after the cold northern Winters and I didn't mind at all because it was always delicious. Countries which grow lemons naturally use them more than we do, so here are some recipes from abroad to round off this chapter – Swedish lemon cream, pork with spicy lemon sauce from Portugal and, from Greece, avgolemono, their egg and lemon soup.

Baked Lemon Pudding

75 g (3 oz) caster sugar	2 large eggs, separated
50 g (2 oz) butter, creamed	15 g ($\frac{1}{2}$ oz) plain flour
1 large lemon	190 ml ($7\frac{1}{2}$ fl oz) milk

Gradually add the caster sugar to the creamed butter. Finely grate the rind from the lemon and squeeze and strain the lemon juice. Add the rind to the creamed mixture. Stir in the egg yolks, flour, lemon juice and milk. Whisk the whites until stiff, then fold them into the mixture. Turn into a buttered 15-cm (6-in) soufflé dish and put the dish in a meat tin filled with 2.5 cm (1 in) water. Bake at 180°C (350°F)/Gas 4 for 45 minutes or until the pudding is firm to the touch. Serve with cream.

Serves 6

Lemon Sauce

2 large lemons	20 ml (4 level teaspoons)
50 g (2 oz) caster sugar	arrowroot

Peel the rind from the lemons, discarding all the white pith. Boil the peel with 125 ml ($\frac{1}{4}$ pint) water for 5 minutes. Strain into a measuring jug and stir in the sugar. Squeeze and strain the lemon juice and add to the jug with enough cold water to make 250 ml ($\frac{1}{2}$ pint). Return the lemon mixture to the pan. Blend the arrowroot with a little of the lemon liquid and bring the remainder to the boil. Pour it on to the blended arrowroot, return to the pan and bring to the boil, stirring all the time until the mixture thickens and clears.

Check that this sauce is sweet enough for your taste and stir in more sugar if necessary. Serve with plain baked sponge puddings.

Serves 6

Lemon Meringue Pie

100 g (4 oz) shortcrust
    pastry (see page 35)

100 g (4 oz) caster sugar
2 large egg yolks

Filling:
2 large lemons
45 ml (3 level tablespoons)
    cornflour
15 g (½ oz) butter

Meringue:
75 g (3 oz) caster sugar
2 large egg whites, stiffly
    whisked

Roll the pastry and use to line an 18-cm (7-in) flan dish. Cover the pastry with greaseproof paper and fill with baking beans. Bake blind at 220°C (425°F)/Gas 7 for 15 minutes or until the pastry is firm but not yet golden. Remove beans and paper and return flan to the oven for a further 5 minutes.

Finely grate the rind from the lemons and squeeze and strain the juice. Mix the cornflour with 125 ml ($\frac{1}{4}$ pint) cold water in a pan; add the lemon rind and juice and bring to the boil, stirring all the time. Remove from the heat and stir in the butter and sugar, then beat in the egg yolks. Pour into the flan case and smooth the top. Whisk half the remaining sugar into the egg whites, then fold in the rest of the sugar. Pile the meringue on to the cooled lemon filling and bake at 180°C (350°F)/Gas 4 for about 15 minutes or until the meringue is crisp and lightly browned.

Serves 8

Roast Lemon Chicken

1.5-kg (3-lb) chicken   50 g (2 oz) butter, melted
1 large lemon   salt and pepper
4 sprigs of thyme

Wipe the chicken inside and out and wipe the lemon skin. Push a skewer several times through the lemon skin into the flesh, then push the lemon into the body of the chicken. Add 2 sprigs of thyme and brush the chicken flesh with melted butter. Sprinkle with salt and pepper and lay the chicken on one side of the breast in a meat tin. Roast at 200°C (400°F)/ Gas 6 for 30 minutes, then turn it on to the other side. You'll find when you come to turn it that the underside of the chicken and the exposed leg are brown. Roast for another 30 minutes to complete the cooking of the legs, then turn the chicken breast upwards and cook for another 30 minutes until the breast is crisp and golden brown. Add the remaining sprigs of thyme for the last 30 minutes. Carve in the usual way. The lemon flavour will have permeated the flesh and the chicken should be moist and delicious.

Serves 8

Lamb and Lemon Fry

8 lamb cutlets
1 medium-sized onion,
   chopped
25 g (1 oz) lamb dripping

125 ml (¼ pint) dry cider
juice of 1 lemon, strained
5 ml (1 level teaspoon)
   ground coriander

Trim the cutlets, if necessary, of excess fat. Fry the onions in the dripping in a frying pan until they are soft. Add the cutlets and brown them on both sides. Pour in the cider and lemon juice and bring to the boil. Reduce the heat and simmer the cutlets for 10 minutes. Stir in the coriander and simmer for another 10 minutes. Serve with boiled rice.

Serves 4

Baked Lemon Soufflé

rind of 1 large lemon, thinly
   pared
250 ml (½ pint) milk
25 g (1 oz) plain flour

30 ml (2 tablespoons)
   double cream
50 g (2 oz) caster sugar
25 g (1 oz) butter, softened
3 large eggs, separated

Put the lemon rind (with all white pith removed) with the milk in a pan. Bring to the boil, then remove from the heat and allow to stand for 30 minutes. Sift the flour into a bowl, pour in the cream and strain in the milk, beating all the time. Return this mixture to the pan, bring to the boil, stirring, and cook it for 1 minute. Beat in the sugar, butter and egg yolks one at a time. Whisk the whites stiffly but not until they are dry and fold them into the soufflé mixture. Turn at once into a buttered 18-cm (7-in) soufflé dish and bake at 200°C (400°F)/Gas 6 for 15–20 minutes until the top is evenly brown and firm to the touch. Serve straight from the oven with cream.

Serves 6

Crispy Lamb Roll

1 large lamb breast, boned,
  weighing 0.75 kg (1¾ lb)

Stuffing:
1 large onion, chopped
25 g (1 oz) lamb dripping
100 g (4 oz) dried apricots,
  chopped

50 g (2 oz) almond nibs,
  toasted
15 ml (1 level tablespoon)
  parsley, roughly chopped
salt and pepper
100 g (4 oz) fresh white
  breadcrumbs
1 large egg, beaten
grated rind of 1 lemon

If you've always thought that breast of lamb is too fatty, try cooking it this way before you write it off as a cut that's not for you. Cut as much fat as possible off the lamb breast and lay it flat on a work surface, skin side down. For the stuffing, cook the onion in the dripping for 5 minutes until it is soft. Mix the dried apricots, almonds, parsley and salt and pepper with the breadcrumbs. Stir in the onion and mix with the beaten egg. Finally stir in the lemon rind and if the stuffing is too dry, squeeze and strain in a little of the lemon juice. Spread this stuffing over the lamb, roll it up and secure it at 2.5-cm (1-in) intervals with clean white string. Put it on the shelf of your oven, placing a meat tin underneath to catch the drips. Roast at 180°C (350°F)/Gas 4 for 1 hour 30 minutes or until the fat is crisp and brown. Cut into thick slices and serve with onion gravy.

Serves 4

Syllabub

1 large lemon
100 g (4 oz) sugar lumps
60 ml (4 tablespoons)
  sherry

30 ml (2 tablespoons)
  brandy
250 ml (½ pint) double
  cream

Wipe the lemon and rub the sugar lumps all over the skin until the sugar has absorbed the oil. Put the sugar in a bowl. Squeeze and strain the lemon juice. Add to the bowl with the sherry and brandy and leave for 2 hours until the sugar has dissolved. Pour on the cream and whisk gently until the mixture thickens. Stop when it leaves soft trails as you raise the whisk; if you beat it any longer the syllabub will develop a grainy appearance. Serve with plain biscuits.

Serves 4

Swedish Lemon Cream

100 g (4 oz) caster sugar   1 large lemon
125 ml (¼ pint) dry white   6 large egg yolks
   wine

Mix the sugar and wine in a saucepan. Finely grate the lemon rind and squeeze and strain the juice. Add rind and juice to the pan with the egg yolks. Heat very gently, stirring all the time, until the cream begins to thicken. Don't let the mixture boil, or the egg yolks will curdle. Remove the pan from the heat when the mixture is thick enough to coat your wooden spoon, and stir the cream until it is cool. Turn it into a serving dish and leave it for 3 hours to set. Chill if you wish, but I think this sweet is nicest at room temperature.

Serves 4

Sole with Lemon Sauce

4 small sole, skinned   25 g (1 oz) plain flour
15 ml (1 level tablespoon)   125 ml (¼ pint) fish stock
   plain flour   125 ml (¼ pint) milk
salt and pepper   1 small lemon
50 g (2 oz) unsalted butter   salt and pepper
                               30 ml (2 tablespoons)
Lemon sauce: single cream
25 g (1 oz) butter

Wipe the fish. Season the flour with salt and pepper and use
to coat the fish. Melt the butter in a large frying pan and
fry the sole (upper side first) for about 5 minutes or until
golden brown, then carefully turn the fish and fry the underside for another 5 minutes or so. You may have to divide
the fish and butter between 2 frying pans if the fish are large.

Make the sauce while the fish are frying. Melt the butter
in a saucepan, stir in the flour and cook the mixture for 1
minute, stirring frequently. Remove from the heat and gradually stir in the fish stock and milk. Return to the heat, bring
to the boil, stirring the sauce all the time, and cook for
2 minutes after the sauce has thickened. Stir frequently.
Finely grate the rind from the lemon and squeeze and strain
the juice. Add rind and juice to the sauce and season with
salt and pepper. Taste at this point; you'll find it quite
sharp so stir in the cream and taste again, adding more
cream or top of the milk and seasoning if necessary.

Serves 4

Lemon Refrigerator Cake

60 ml (4 tablespoons)
    brandy
213-g (7½-oz) packet semi-
    sweet biscuits
75 g (3 oz) butter
125 g (5 oz) caster sugar
4 large eggs, separated

1 large lemon
142-g (5-oz) carton double
    cream, whipped
25 g (1 oz) plain
    chocolate, melted
25 g (1 oz) flaked almonds,
    toasted

Pour the brandy into a dish, dip a few biscuits into it and
use them to line the base of an 18-cm (7-in) cake tin previously
lined with a circle of greaseproof paper. Don't fill the gaps
in the biscuits. Ideally choose the size tin which will take a
ring of whole biscuits plus one in the centre, because this
cake is turned out of the tin. Cream the butter and sugar
until it's very fluffy. Beat the egg yolks, one at a time, into

the butter cream. Finely grate the lemon rind and squeeze and strain the juice. Beat in the rind and juice. Whisk the egg whites stiffly and fold them into the creamed mixture. Spoon a third of this over the biscuits in the tin and smooth the surface. Dip more biscuits in brandy and arrange them as before, then continue layering the butter cream and biscuits, finishing with a circle of biscuits. Cover the tin and leave it in the fridge for 24 hours.

Remove the cake from the tin and peel off the grease-proof paper. Decorate it with piped cream. Drizzle chocolate over the top by dipping a fork in it and letting it run off the tines all over the cake. Sprinkle with the almonds.

Serves 10–12

Lemon Walnut Slices

100 g (4 oz) soft, whipped tub margarine
100 g (4 oz) caster sugar
2 small lemons
2 large eggs
100 g (4 oz) self-raising flour
50 g (2 oz) unsalted butter, softened

200 g (8 oz) icing sugar, sifted
15 ml (1 tablespoon) hot water
yellow colouring
walnut halves

Put the margarine and caster sugar into a mixing bowl. Finely grate the rind from both lemons and squeeze and strain the juice. Add all the rind and half the juice to the bowl with the eggs and flour. Beat well together for 2 minutes by hand, less if using an electric mixer. Spoon the mixture into a greased 15-cm (6-in) square cake tin with a fixed base. Bake at 180°C (350°F)/Gas 4 for about 40 minutes or until the sponge is springy to touch and has shrunk slightly away from the sides of the tin. Turn on to a wire rack to cool, then cut the sponge into two layers.

Beat the butter with 100 g (4 oz) icing sugar until it is light and fluffy. Beat in half the remaining lemon juice. Cut the cake into 12 2.5-cm (1-in) pieces. Sandwich the 2 layers of each cake with the butter cream. Stir the hot water and remaining lemon juice into the remaining icing sugar and colour it a pale creamy yellow with colouring. Coat the top of each cake with icing and press a walnut half into each cake before the icing sets.

Makes 12

Lemon Barley Water

100 g (4 oz) pearl barley   4 large lemons
100 g (4 oz) caster sugar

Put the barley in a saucepan, cover it with cold water and bring to the boil. Strain and rinse the barley under running cold water. Return it to the pan, add 1 litre (2 pints) cold water and bring to the boil. Cover the pan and simmer the barley for 1½ hours. Strain the liquid into a large jug, stir in the sugar and allow to cool. Finely grate the lemon rind and squeeze and strain the juice. Stir both into the barley water and leave to stand for 2 hours before drinking. If you don't like the bits of lemon rind, strain it again before serving.

Makes 1 litre (2 pints)

Cheesecake

2 550-ml (1-pint) packets   142-g (5-oz) carton double
   lemon jelly   cream, whipped
250 ml (½ pint) milk
2 large eggs, separated   *Crumb base:*
2 large lemons   100 g (4 oz) ginger biscuits
450 g (1 lb) cottage cheese   50 g (2 oz) butter, melted

Pull the jelly into sections and put in a pan with 125 ml (¼ pint) cold water. Heat slowly, stirring occasionally, until the jelly has dissolved. Whisk the milk with the egg yolks and pour it into the jelly, then return the pan to the heat and cook it gently for 2 minutes but without letting it boil, which could cause curdling. Finely grate the rind from the lemons and squeeze and strain the juice. Add rind and juice to the jelly. Blend the jelly and cottage cheese in batches to a smooth purée. Whisk the egg whites stiffly, then fold the cream followed by the egg whites into the mixture when it's cool. Line the base of a 20-cm (8-in) cake tin with a fixed base with a round of greaseproof paper. Pour in the mixture and leave it to set.

For the base, crush the ginger biscuits fairly finely. Stir in the melted butter. Cover the cheesecake, pressing the crumbs on lightly. Leave in the fridge to chill, then turn out the cheesecake on to its crumb coating. Run a knife dipped in hot water around the edge of the tin to loosen the mixture from the sides if it seems stubborn. Peel off the paper and decorate if liked with more whipped cream, angelica or toasted almond flakes.

Serves 8

Lemonade

4 large lemons
225 g (8 oz) granulated
  sugar

1 litre (2 pints) boiling
  water

Pare the rind from the lemons and put it with the sugar in a large bowl. Pour on the boiling water and leave to cool, stirring now and then. Squeeze and strain the lemon juice and add it to the bowl. Strain into a jug and serve chilled.

Makes 1·25 litres (2½ pints)

Lemon Water Ice

1.5 kg (3 lb) granulated   8 large lemons
  sugar   2 large egg whites, whisked

Put the sugar with 750 ml (1½ pints) cold water in a heavy
pan. Bring slowly to the boil, making sure the sugar has
dissolved before boiling point is reached, then boil gently
for 10 minutes. Remove any scum, and strain. Pare the rind
from the lemons, discarding any white pith..Put the rind in a
basin and cover it with the hot sugar syrup. Allow to cool,
covered. Squeeze and strain the juice from the lemons and
add it to the basin. Strain into freezing trays or cake tins
and freeze until the ice is mushy round the edges. Turn it
into a bowl, beat well, then fold in the stiffly beaten egg
whites. Return to the tins and freeze completely.

Serves 8

Avgolemono (Greek Egg and Lemon Soup)

2 large chicken joints   3 large eggs, beaten
1 small onion, skinned   juice of 2 large lemons,
1 celery top   strained
salt and pepper   5 ml (1 level teaspoon)
50 g (2 oz) long-grain rice   mint, chopped

Put the chicken, onion and celery top in a saucepan. Add
1.75 litres (3 pints) cold water and a good pinch each of salt
and pepper. Bring to the boil, cover and simmer gently
for 2 hours. When it is cooked, lift out the chicken and strain
the stock. Cut the chicken meat into small pieces and keep
on one side. Return the stock to the rinsed pan, add the
rice and cook it for about 13 minutes. Add 30 ml (2 tablespoons) cold water to the eggs and beat in the lemon juice
until the mixture is frothy. Take a ladleful of hot stock, and,

stirring all the time, pour it slowly on to the eggs. Add
another ladleful, stirring, then pour this back into the pan,
stirring all the time. Don't let the soup boil now or the eggs
will curdle. Add the chicken pieces and the mint and serve
at once.

Serves 6–8

Chicken in Lemon Jelly

2 550-ml (1-pint) packets
    lemon jelly
675 ml (1¼ pints) boiling
    water
2 large lemons
100 g (4 oz) black grapes,
    halved

100 g (4 oz) white grapes,
    halved
175 g (6 oz) cooked
    chicken, chopped

Dissolve the jellies in the boiling water. Squeeze and strain
the lemon juice and stir it into the jelly. Rinse a 15-cm (6-in)
cake tin with a fixed base and pour 1.25 cm (½ in) liquid
jelly into it. Leave it to set. Cool the remaining jelly but
don't let it set. If it looks on the point of doing so, stir it
over a pan of very hot water until it liquefies again. Remove
the pips from the grapes. Dip the grape halves in the liquid
jelly, arrange them on the set jelly in a pattern and leave to
set. When set, pour a layer of liquid jelly over the decorations and leave to set again. Mix 30 ml (2 tablespoons) liquid
jelly with the chicken and any remaining grape halves and
spoon this into the tin. (If you're feeling really artistic, you
could decorate the sides of the cake tin with grapes by
dipping them and allowing them to set in place before
adding any other ingredients.) When the chicken has set,
fill the tin with some of the remaining jelly and allow it to
set. Turn out the chicken and if you have any jelly left over,
chop it when set using a knife dipped in boiling water. This

will preserve the brilliance of the jelly. Surround the chicken
with chopped jelly and serve with salads.

Serves 4

Pork with Spicy Lemon Sauce

0.5 kg (1 lb) blade of pork
15 g (½ oz) lard
125 ml (¼ pint) dry white
    wine
10 ml (1 level dessertspoon)
    ground cumin

1 clove garlic, crushed
salt and pepper
3 thin slices of lemon
5 ml (1 level teaspoon)
    ground coriander

Cut the meat into 5-cm (1-in) cubes and heat the lard in a
frying pan. Add the meat and brown it on all sides, turning
it frequently. Stir in 90 ml (6 tablespoons) wine, the cumin,
garlic, 3 ml (½ level teaspoon) salt and sprinkle with freshly
ground pepper. Bring to the boil, then simmer for 55 minutes
or until the pork is tender. Add the remaining wine. Cut the
lemon slices into quarters and add to the pan. Cook for 2
minutes. Stir in the coriander, cook for 2 minutes more and
serve at once with rice.

Serves 4

Fresh Lemon Jelly Whip

2 large lemons
50 g (2 oz) caster sugar

25 g (1 oz) powdered
    gelatine

Peel the rind from the lemons, leaving all the white pith on
the fruit. If there's any pith on the rind, cut it off. Put the
rind with 500 ml (1 pint) cold water in a pan and simmer it
for 10 minutes. Remove the rind by straining and stir the

sugar in the water until dissolved. Dissolve the gelatine by putting it in a basin with 60 ml (4 tablespoons) cold water and standing the basin in a pan of gently simmering water. Squeeze and strain the lemon juice and stir it into the lemon-flavoured water with the gelatine. When on the point of setting, whisk the jelly to a thick foam. Pour into individual moulds and leave to set.

Serves 6

Soufflé Milanaise

3 large eggs, separated
1 large lemon
15 g (½ oz) powdered
   gelatine
100 g (4 oz) caster sugar
142-g (5-oz) carton double
   cream

142-g (5-oz) carton single
   cream
50 g (2 oz) almond nibs,
   toasted
angelica

Cut a piece of greaseproof paper long enough to go round a 13-cm (5-in) soufflé dish and wide enough to stand 5 cm (2 in) higher than the dish. Grease the paper lightly with butter and secure the paper round the dish with Sellotape.

Put the egg yolks in a large bowl. Finely grate the lemon rind into the bowl, then squeeze and strain the lemon juice into the bowl. Put the gelatine in a basin with 30 ml (2 tablespoons) cold water, stand the basin in a pan of hot water and leave it to dissolve. Add the sugar to the egg yolks and lemon and stand the bowl over a pan of hot water, making sure the base of the bowl doesn't touch the water. Whisk for 10 to 15 minutes until the mixture is creamy light and the whisk will leave a trail in the mixture. Remove the bowl from the heat and whisk until it has cooled. Trickle in the gelatine (do this by pouring it in a thin stream from a height of 60 cm (2 feet), so that if the gelatine is a little too hot, it cools on its way from basin to bowl). Whisk the mixture all the time you're adding the gelatine.

Whip the creams together until they form soft peaks. Whisk the egg whites stiffly but not to the dry stage – you'll find them difficult to fold in smoothly if they're really dry. Fold the cream and then the egg whites into the lemon mixture, using a large metal spoon. Turn the mixture into the soufflé dish and leave to set. I think it's best left to set naturally – the fridge seems to toughen gelatine mixtures and it's the gelatine that sets the soufflé, not the cold.

When the soufflé is set, carefully remove the paper by dipping a palette knife in hot water and, holding one edge against the soufflé, moving it around the edge as you peel off the paper. If you hold the knife against the paper you'll find the soufflé comes away in lumps. If the edge of your soufflé is perfect, show it off and leave it plain. If it's not smooth, coat it with the toasted almond nibs. Decorate the top with angelica diamond-shapes and some extra whipped cream, piped on in tiny rosettes.

Serves 8

Index

Chocolate
  Butter Cream, 105
  Cherry Cases, 95
  Choc-nut Cherry Cake, 99
  Cream Icing, 101
  Frosting, 105
  Little Chocolate Rolls, 105
  Orange Mousse, 88
  Sponge Layer, 101
  Surprise Soufflé, 86
  Yo-yos, 103
Cider Sauce, 58
Cockles
  and Bacon, 60
  Cod and Cockle Pie, 63
Coconut Pyramids, 119
Cod
  and Cockle Pie, 63
  Curried, 62
  Fish Crumble, 58
  Russian Cod Pie, 53
Coffee Milk Jelly, 86
Coleslaw, 41
Coley
  Fish Cakes, 51
  Mousseline, 56
Courgettes
  Boiled, 26
  Cheesy Baked, 27
  Vinaigrette, 27
Creamy Garlic Sauce, 48
Crêpes, Apple, 131
Crêpes Suzette, 132
Crudité, 44
Cucumber Salad, 41
Curried Cod, 62
Custard, Real, 121
Custard Tart, 117

Dressings
  Aïoli, 47
  Blender Mayonnaise, 47

Fatless Sponge, 101
Fish (*see also* under individual names)
  Cakes, 51
  Crumble, 58
  Mousseline of, 56
Flan, Orange Apple, 96
  Asparagus, 35
Floating Islands, 119
Florentine Brill, 55
Fool, Rhubarb, 84
Fritters
  Artichoke, 21
  Banana, 135
  Gooseberry, 133
Fruity Batter Pudding, 132

Gammon in Puff Pastry, 75
Genoese Sponge, 99
Ginger Rhubarb Jam, 152
Gooseberry
  Almond Tarts, 96
  Crumble, 85
  Fritters, 133
  Jam, 153
  Relish, 151
  Sauce, 52
Grapefruit in Brandy, 89
Greek Easter Bread, 142
Greek Easter Lamb, 148
Green Salad, 39

Haddock, Buttered Eggs with, 116
Honeycomb Mould, 94
Hot Cross Buns, 140

Italian Easter Cake, 145

Jam and Cream Sponge, 105
Jerusalem Artichokes, *see* Artichokes

Lamb
  and Lemon Fry, 162
  Cream Roast, 71